Published by
Rajneesh Foundation International
Rajneeshpuram, Oregon 97741 U.S.A.

Tantra
Spirituality
& Sex

Bhagwan Shree Rajneesh

Editor: Ma Yoga Anurag
Design: Ma Anand Zeno
Direction: Ma Yoga Pratima, M.M., D.Phil., Arihanta
Copyright: ©1983 Rajneesh Foundation International
Published by: Ma Anand Sheela, M.M., D.Phil.,
              D. Litt., Acharya
              Rajneesh Foundation International
              P.O. Box 9, Rajneeshpuram
              Oregon 97741, U.S.A.

First Edition: 1977 U.S.A. Rainbow Bridge—10,000 copies
Second Edition: September 1983—40,000 copies

Pages 372-388 from THE BOOK OF THE SECRETS,
Volume 2 by Bhagwan Shree Rajneesh
Copyright ©1975 by Rajneesh Foundation International
Reprinted by permission of Harper & Row, Publishers, Inc.

Pages 3-22, 25-43, 338-341 from THE BOOK OF THE
SECRETS, Volume 3 by Bhagwan Shree Rajneesh
Copyright ©1976 by Rajneesh Foundation International
Reprinted by permission of Harper & Row, Publishers, Inc.

The sutras quoted in this book are taken from
Zen Flesh, Zen Bones (ed. Penguin, 1972 reprint)
translated and compiled by Paul Reps.

Printed in U.S.A.
ISBN 0-88050-696-2 (previously ISBN 0-914-198-11-4)
Library of Congress Catalog Number 83-16036

CONTENTS

Each of the chapters in this book has been taken from the series
The Book of the Secrets (5 volumes)—
chapter one: from volume 1, chapter 2, given October 2, 1972
chapter two: from volume 1, chapter 7, given October 7, 1972
chapter three: from volume 3, chapter 14, given March 30, 1973
chapter four: from volume 3, chapter 1, given February 22, 1973
chapter five: from volume 3, chapter 2, given February 23, 1973
chapter six: from volume 2, chapter 16, given January 29, 1973

INTRODUCTION

The introduction to this book should be a song, or a dance, or a melting sunset on a warm summer's evening. The experience you will encounter through its pages defies description. Bhagwan Shree Rajneesh is a living Master, whose very presence is a confirmation of the vital truth each one of us carries within our hearts.

Somehow, in the frenzy of the twentieth century we have been blinded to our own natures. The world has become an alien and artificial place where neurosis and frustration abound, where anger and violence simmer below a veneer of conformity, ready to erupt at any moment.

In opening for us the world of Tantra, Bhagwan goes to the root cause of our modern malaise. Sex is the most basic energy. It permeates every cell of our being. It is our source. Yet so often it is treated from a place of control, either as an energy to be repressed or as a means of dominating and exploiting others.

Bhagwan, in His unique style, breaks the mold. With clarity and profound insight He opens the door to our authentic being. There is nothing other-worldly in His vision. It is rooted in the earth. The starting point is here-now, and the key is an acceptance of ourselves as we are. In that acceptance is transformation. This is the wonderful secret of Tantra that Bhagwan shares. Accept desire, move with it, but in a deep sensitivity, with awareness, with love.

"Sex is just the beginning, not the end.
But if you miss the beginning you will
miss the end also."

Don't miss! Let His words resonate in your heart. Let a great trust arise. Let Him carry you along in the joyous adventure of life.

Swami Premgeet
August 1983

The material in this book is taken from
discourses given by Bhagwan Shree Rajneesh,
based on the Vigyan Bhairava Tantra and in
response to questions from disciples and
visitors during 1972 & 1973 in Bombay, India.

Tantra and Yoga

"Sex is the basic energy. . .
For Yoga, fight with this energy. . .
For Tantra, use it, transform it!"

Many questions are there. The first:

> *Bhagwan, what is the difference between traditional Yoga and Tantra. Are they the same?*

TANTRA AND YOGA are basically different. They reach to the same goal, but the paths are not only different but contrary also. So this has to be understood very clearly.

The Yoga process is also methodology, Yoga is also technique. Yoga is not philosophy. Just like Tantra, Yoga also depends on action, method, technique. Doing leads to being in Yoga also, but the process is different. In Yoga one has to fight; that is the path of the warrior. On the path of Tantra one has not to fight at all. Rather, on the contrary, one has to indulge, but with awareness.

1

Yoga is suppression with awareness, Tantra is indulgence with awareness.

Tantra says that whatsoever you are, the ultimate is not opposite to it. It is a growth; you can grow to be the ultimate. There is no opposition between you and the reality. You are part of it, so no struggle, no conflict, no opposition to nature is needed. You have to use nature, you have to use whatsoever you are to go beyond.

In Yoga, you have to fight with yourself to go beyond. In Yoga, the world and the *moksha*, you as you are and you as you can be, are two opposite things. Suppress, fight, dissolve that which you are so that you can attain that which you can be. Going beyond in Yoga is a death. You must die for your real being to be born. In the eyes of Tantra, Yoga is a deep suicide: you must kill your natural self—your body, your instincts, your desires, everything.

Tantra says accept yourself as you are. It is a deep acceptance. Don't create a gap between you and the real, between the world and the nirvana. Don't create any gap! There is no gap for Tantra. No death is needed. For your rebirth, no death is needed; rather, a transcendence. For this transcendence, *use* yourself.

For example, sex is there, the basic energy—the basic energy you are born through, born with. The basic cells of your being, of your body, are sexual, so the human mind revolves around sex. For Yoga, fight with this energy. Through fight, you create a different center in yourself. The more you fight, the more you become integrated on a different center. Then sex is not your center.

Fighting with sex—of course, consciously—will create a new center in you of being, a new emphasis, a new crystallization. Then sex will not be your energy. You will create your energy fighting with sex. A different energy will come into being, and a different center of existence.

For Tantra, use the energy of sex, don't fight with it. Transform it! Don't think in terms of enmity; be friendly to it. It is *your* energy; it is not evil, it is not bad. Every energy is just neutral. It can be used against you, it can be used for you. You can make a block of it, a barrier; you can make a step. It can be used. Rightly used, it becomes friendly. Wrongly used, it becomes your enemy. It is neither. Energy is neutral.

As ordinary man is using sex, it becomes your enemy; it destroys you. You simply dissipate in it. Yoga takes the opposite view, opposite to the

3

ordinary mind. The ordinary mind is being destroyed by its own desires. So Yoga says stop desiring, be desireless! Fight desire and create an integration in you which is desireless.

Tantra says be aware of the desire. Don't create any fight. Move in desire with full consciousness. And when you move in desire with full consciousness, you transcend it. You are in it and still you are not in it. You pass through it, but you remain an outsider.

Yoga appealed much because Yoga is just opposite to the ordinary mind. So the ordinary mind can understand the language of Yoga. You know how sex is destroying you, how it has destroyed you, how you go on revolving around it like a slave, like a puppet. You know this by your experience. So when Yoga says fight it, you immediately understand the language. That is the appeal, easy appeal of Yoga.

Tantra could not be so easily appealing. It seems difficult: how to move in desire without being overwhelmed by it? How to be in the sex act consciously, with full awareness? The ordinary mind becomes afraid; it seems dangerous. Not that it is dangerous: whatsoever you know about sex creates this danger for you. You know yourself, you know how you can deceive yourself. You know very well that your mind is cunning. You can move in desire, in sex, in everything, and you can deceive yourself that you are moving with full awareness. That's why you feel the danger. The danger is not in Tantra, it is in you. And the appeal of Yoga is because of you, your ordinary mind, your sex-suppressed, sex-starved, sex-indulging mind.

Because the ordinary mind is not healthy about sex, Yoga has appeal. A better humanity, with a healthy sex—natural, normal. . . We are not normal and natural. We are absolutely abnormal, unhealthy, really insane. But because everyone is like us, we never feel it. Madness is so normal that not to be mad may look abnormal. A Buddha is abnormal, a Jesus is abnormal, amidst us. They don't belong to us. This normalcy is a disease.

This "normal" mind has created the appeal of Yoga. If you take sex naturally, with no philosophy around it, with no philosophy for or against; if you take sex as you take your hands, your eyes, if it is totally accepted as a natural thing, then Tantra will have appeal, and then only can Tantra be useful for many.

But the days of Tantra are coming. Sooner or

later Tantra is going to explode for the first time on the masses, because for the first time the time is ripe—ripe to take sex naturally. It is possible that explosion may come from the West, because Freud, Jung, Reich, they have prepared the background. They don't know anything about Tantra, but they have made the basic ground for Tantra to evolve.

Western psychology has come to a conclusion that the basic human disease is somewhere around sex, the basic insanity of man is sex-oriented. So unless this sex orientation is dissolved, man cannot be natural, normal. Man has gone wrong only because of attitudes about sex.

No attitude is needed—only then are you natural. What attitude have you about your eyes? Are they evil or are they divine? Are you for your eyes or against them? No attitude! That's why your eyes are normal. Take some attitude, think that eyes are evil, then seeing will become difficult. Then seeing will take the same problematic shape as sex has taken. Then you would like to see. You will desire and you will hanker to see. But when you see you will feel guilty; whenever you see you will feel guilty. You have done something wrong, you have sinned. You would like to kill the very instrument of seeing; you would like to destroy your eyes. And the more you want to destroy them, the more you will become eye-centered. Then you will start a very absurd activity: you would like more and more to see, and simultaneously you will feel more and more guilty. The same has happened with the sex center.

Tantra says accept whatsoever you are. This is the basic note—total acceptance. And only through total acceptance can you grow. Then use every energy you have. How can you use them? Accept them, then find out what these energies are. What is sex? What is this phenomenon? We are not acquainted with it. We know many things about sex taught by others. We may have passed through the sex act, but with a guilty mind, with a suppressive attitude, in haste, in hurry. Something has to be done and unburdened. The sex act is not a loving act. You are not happy in it, but you cannot leave it. The more you try to leave it, the more attractive it becomes. The more you want to negate it, the more you feel invited.

You cannot negate it, but this attitude to negate, to destroy, destroys the very mind, the very awareness, the very sensibility, which can under-

7

stand it. So sex goes on with no sensitivity in it. Then you cannot understand. Only deep sensitivity can understand anything. A deep feeling, a deep moving in it, can understand anything. You can understand sex only if you move in it as a poet moves amidst flowers—only then. If you feel guilty about flowers, you may pass through the garden but you will pass with closed eyes and you will be in a hurry—in a deep mad haste. Somehow you have to go out of the garden. Then how can you be aware?

So Tantra says: Accept whatsoever you are—a great mystery of many multi-dimensional energies. Accept it, and move with every energy with deep sensitivity, with awareness, with love, with understanding. Move with it. . .then every desire becomes a vehicle to go beyond it. Then every energy becomes a help, and then this very world is nirvana, and then this very body is a temple, a holy temple, a holy place.

Yoga is negation, Tantra is affirmation. Yoga thinks in terms of duality; that's why the word 'yoga'. It means to put two things together, to yoke two things together. But two things are there, the duality is there.

Tantra says there is no duality. If there is duality, then you cannot put them together. And howsoever you try, they will remain two; howsoever put together, they will remain two. And the fight will continue and the dualism will remain. If the world and the divine are two, then they cannot be put together. If really they are *not* two, they are only appearing as two, only then can they be one. If your body and soul are two, then they cannot be put together. If you and the God are two, then there is no possibility of putting them together. They will remain two.

Tantra says there is no duality; it is only an appearance. So why help appearance to grow more? Tantra says, why help this appearance of duality to grow more? Dissolve it this very moment! Be one! Through acceptance you become one, not through fight. Accept the world, accept the body, accept everything that is inherent in it. Don't create a different center in yourself, because for Tantra that different center is nothing but the ego. For Tantra, remember, that is nothing but the ego. Don't create an ego; just be aware what you are. If you fight, then the ego will be there. So it is difficult to find a yogi who is not an egoist. It is difficult! And Yogis may go on talking about egolessness, but they cannot be egoless.

Their very process creates the ego. The fight is the process. If you fight you are bound to create an ego. And the more you fight, the more strengthened the ego will be. And if you win in your fight, then you will achieve the supreme ego.

Tantra says no fight! Then there is no possibility of the ego. If we understand Tantra then there will be many problems, because for us if there is no fight there is only indulgence. No fight means indulgence for us, and then we become afraid. We have indulged for lives together and we have reached nowhere. But for Tantra, indulgence is not our indulgence. Tantra says: Indulge, but be aware. You are angry; Tantra will not say don't be angry. Tantra says be angry, wholeheartedly, but be aware! Tantra is not against anger, Tantra is only against spiritual sleepiness, spiritual unconsciousness. Be aware and be angry. And this is the secret of the method, that if you are aware, anger is transformed. It becomes compassion.

So Tantra says: Don't say anger is your enemy —it is compassion in seed. The same anger, the same energy, will become compassion. If you fight with it, then there will be no possibility for compassion. So if you succeed in fighting, in suppressing, you will be a dead man. There will be no anger because you have suppressed it. There will be no compassion either, because only anger can be transformed into compassion. If you succeed in your suppression—which is impossible— then there will be no sex but no love either, because with sex dead there is no energy to grow into love. So you will be without sex, but you will be also without love. And then the whole point is missed, because without love there is no divineness and without love there is no liberation and without love there is no freedom.

Tantra says these same energies are to be transformed. It can be said in this way: if you are against the world then there is no nirvana, because this world itself is to be transformed into nirvana. Then you are against the basic energies which are the source. So Tantra alchemy says don't fight; be friendly with all the energies that are given to you. Welcome them. Feel grateful that you have anger, that you have sex, that you have greed. Feel grateful because these are the hidden sources. And they can be transformed and they can be opened. And when sex is transformed, it becomes love. The poison is lost, the ugliness is lost.

The seed is ugly, but when it becomes alive, sprouts and flowers, then there is beauty. Don't throw the seed, because you are also throwing the flowers in it. They are not there yet, not yet manifest so that you can see them. They are unmanifest, but they *are* there. Use this seed so that you can attain to flowers. Acceptance, a sensitive understanding and awareness—then indulgence is allowed.

One thing more, which is really very strange, but one of the deepest discoveries of Tantra. And that is: whatsoever you take as your enemies—greed, anger, hate, sex, whatsoever—your attitude that they are enemies makes them your enemies. Take them as divine gifts and approach them with a very grateful heart.

For example, Tantra has developed many techniques for the transformation of sex energy. Approach the sexual act as if you are approaching the temple of the divine. Approach the sexual act as if it is prayer, as if it is meditation. Feel the holiness of it. That's why in Khajuraho, in Puri, in Konarak, every temple has *maithun* sculptures. The sex act on the walls of temples seems illogical, particularly for Christianity, for Islam, for Jainism. It seems inconceivable, contradictory.

How is the temple joined with *maithun* pictures? On the outer walls of the Khajuraho temples, every conceivable type of sexual act is pictured in stone. Why? In a temple it doesn't have any place, in our minds at least. Christianity cannot conceive a church wall with Khajuraho pictures. Impossible!

Modern Hindus also feel guilty because modern Hindus' minds are created by Christianity. They are Hindu-Christians, and they are worse— because to be a Christian is good, but to be a Hindu-Christian is just weird. They feel guilty. One Hindu leader, Purshottamdas Tandan, even proposed that these temples should be destroyed. They don't belong to us! Really, they don't belong to us because Tantra has not been in our hearts for a long time, for centuries. It has not been the main current. Yoga has been the main current, and for Yoga, Khajuraho is inconceivable. It must be destroyed.

Tantra says approach the sex act as if you are entering a holy temple. That's why they pictured the sex act on their holy temples. They said approach sex as if you are entering a holy temple. So when you enter a holy temple, sex must be there so they become conjoined in your mind, associated, so that you can feel the world and the divine are not two fighting elements, but one. They are not contradictory, but polar opposites helping each other. And they can exist only because of this polarity. If this polarity is lost, this whole world is lost. So see the deep-running oneness. Don't see the polar points only, see the inner running current which makes them one.

For Tantra, everything is holy. Remember this: for Tantra *everything* is holy, nothing is unholy. Look at it in this way: for an irreligious person, everything is unholy. For so-called religious persons, something is holy, something unholy. For Tantra, everything is holy.

One Christian missionary was with me some days before and he said, "God created the world." So I asked him, "Who created sin?" He said, "The Devil." Then I asked him, "Who created the Devil?" Then he was at a loss. He said, "Of course, God created the Devil." The Devil creates sin and God creates the Devil. Then who is the real sinner—the Devil or God? But a dualist conception always leads to such absurdities.

For Tantra, God and the Devil are not two. Really, for Tantra, there is nothing which can be called 'the Devil'. Everything is divine, everything is holy! And this seems the right standpoint, the deepest. If anything is unholy in this world, from where does it come and how can it be?

So only two alternatives are there. First the alternative of the atheist who says everything is unholy, then it is okay. He is also a non-dualist. He sees no holiness in the world. Or the Tantra alternative: everything is holy. He is again a non-dualist. But between these two, the so-called religious persons are not really religious—neither religious nor irreligious—because then they are always in a conflict. And their whole theology is just trying to make ends meet, and those ends cannot meet.

If a single cell, a single atom in this world is unholy, then the whole world becomes unholy—because how can that single atom exist in a holy world? How can it be! It is supported by everything. To be, it has to be supported by everything. And if the unholy element is supported by all the holy elements, then what is the difference? So either the world is holy totally, unconditionally, or it is unholy. There is no middle path.

Tantra says everything is holy—that's why we cannot understand it. It is the deepest non-dual standpoint, if we can call it a standpoint. It is not, because any standpoint is bound to be dual. It is not against anything, so it is not a standpoint. It is a felt unity, a lived unity.

These are two paths—Yoga and Tantra. Tantra could not be so appealing because of our crippled minds. But whenever there is someone who is healthy inside, not a chaos, Tantra has a beauty. Then only can he understand what Tantra is. Yoga has appeal, easy appeal, because of our disturbed minds. Remember, it is ultimately *your* mind which makes anything attractive or not attractive. It is you who are the deciding factor.

These approaches are different. I am not saying that one cannot reach through Yoga. One can reach through Yoga also, but not through the Yoga which is prevalent. The Yoga which is prevalent is really not Yoga but your interpretation, of the diseased mind.

Yoga can be authentically an approach towards the ultimate, but that too is only possible when your mind is healthy, when your mind is not diseased and ill. Then Yoga takes a different shape. For example, Mahavira is on the path of Yoga, but he is not really suppressing sex—because he has known, he has lived. He is deeply acquainted with it and it has become useless, so it drops. Buddha is on the path of Yoga, but he has lived through the world; he is deeply acquainted with it. He is not fighting.

Once you know something, you become free of it. It simply drops like dead leaves dropping from a tree. It is not renunciation; there is no fight involved at all. Look at Buddha's face—it doesn't look the face of a fighter. He has not been fighting. He is so relaxed! His face is the very symbol of relaxation. . .no fight.

Look at your yogis: the fight is apparent on their faces. Deep down, much turmoil is there. Just now they are sitting on volcanoes. You can look in their eyes, in their faces, and you will feel it—deep down somewhere they have suppressed all their diseases. But they have not gone beyond.

In a healthy world where everyone is living his life authentically, individually, not imitating others, living his own life in his own way, both Yoga and Tantra are possible. One may learn the deep sensitivity which transcends; one may come to a point where all desires become futile and drop. Yoga can also lead to this, but to me, Yoga will lead also in the same world in which Tantra can lead—remember this.

We need a healthy mind, a natural man. In that

world where natural man is, Tantra will lead and Yoga will also lead. In our so-called ill society, neither Yoga can lead nor Tantra because if we choose Yoga, we don't choose it because desires have become useless—no! They are still meaningful. They are not dropping by themselves. We have to force them.

If we choose Yoga, we choose it as a technique of suppression. If we choose Tantra, we choose it as a cunningness, as a deep deception, to indulge. So with an unhealthy mind neither Yoga nor Tantra—they both will lead to deceptions. A healthy mind, particularly a sexually healthy mind, is needed to start with. Then it is not very difficult to choose your path. You can choose Yoga, you can choose Tantra.

There are two types of persons: basically male and female—not biologically, but psychologically. Those who are basically psychologically male—aggressive, violent, extrovert—Yoga is their path. Those who are basically feminine—receptive, passive, non-violent—Tantra is their path.

So you may note it. For Tantra, the mother, Kali, Tara and so many *devis, bhairavis,* they are very significant. In Yoga, you will never hear any name mentioned of a feminine deity. Tantra has feminine deities, Yoga male gods. Yoga is energy outgoing, Tantra is energy moving inwards. So you can say, in modern psychological terms, Yoga is extrovert and Tantra is introvert. So it depends on the personality. If you have an introvert personality, then fight is not for you. If you have an extrovert personality, then fight is for you.

But we are confused, just confused; we are just a mess. That's why nothing helps. On the contrary, everything disturbs. Yoga will disturb you, Tantra will disturb you, every medicine is going to create a new illness for you, because the chooser is ill, diseased, his choice is ill, diseased.

So I don't mean that through Yoga you cannot reach. I emphasize Tantra only because we are going to understand what Tantra is.

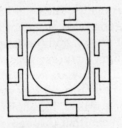

Meditation Techniques: Tantric Love

Shiva says to Devi:
"While being caressed,
sweet princess,
enter the loving
as everlasting life."

S HIVA starts with love. The first technique is concerned with love—because love is the nearest thing, in your experience, in which you are relaxed. If you cannot love, it is impossible for you to relax. If you can relax, your life will become a loving life.

A tense man cannot love. Why? A tense man always lives with purpose. He can earn money, but he cannot love because love is purposeless. Love is not a commodity. You cannot accumulate it; you cannot make a bank balance of it; you cannot strengthen your ego out of it. Really love is the most absurd act—with no meaning beyond it, no purpose beyond it. It exists in itself, not for anything else.

You earn money for something; it is a means. You make a house, you build a house for something, to live in it; it is a means. Love is not a means. Why do you love? For what do you love? Love is the end in itself. That's why a mind that is calculative, logical, a mind that thinks in terms of purpose, cannot love. And a mind that always thinks in terms of purpose will be tense because purpose can only be fulfilled in the future, never here and now.

You build a house; you cannot live in it just now. You will have to build it first. You can live in it in the future, not now. You earn money; the bank balance will be created in the future, not now. Means you will have to use now, and ends will come in the future.

Love is always here. There is no future to it. That's why love is no near to meditation. That's why death is also so near to meditation—because death is always here and now. It can never happen in the future. Can you die in the future? You can die only in the present. No one has ever died in the future. How can you die in the future, or how can you die in the past? The past has gone, it is no more, so you cannot die in it. The future has yet not come, so how can you die in it? Death always occurs in the present.

Death, love, meditation, they all occur in the present. So if you are afraid of death, you cannot love. If you are afraid of love, you cannot meditate. If you are afraid of meditation, your life will be useless—useless not in the sense of any purpose, useless in the sense that you can never feel any bliss in it. . .futile.

It may seem strange to connect these three: love, meditation, death. It is not. They *are* similar experiences. So if you can enter in one, you can enter in the remaining two.

Shiva starts with love. He says:

> *While being caressed,* loved, *sweet princess, enter the caressing,* the loving, *as everlasting life.*

What does it mean? Many things. One, while you are loved past has ceased, future is not. You move in the dimension of the present, you move in the now. Have you ever loved someone? If you have ever loved, then mind is no more there. That's why the so-called wise men say lovers are

23

blind, mindless, mad. They say rightly, in a sense. Lovers are blind because they have no eyes for the future to calculate what they are doing. They are blind! They cannot see the past.

What has happened to lovers? They just move here and now without any consideration of past or future, without any consideration of consequences; that's why they are called blind. They are. They are blind for those who are calculating, and they are seers for those who are not calculating. Those who are not calculating will see love as the real eye, the real vision.

So the first thing: in the moment of love, past and future are no more. One delicate point to be understood: when there is no past and no future, can you call this moment the present? It is the present only between these two—past and future. It is relative. If there is no past and no future, what does it mean to call it the present? It is meaningless. That's why Shiva doesn't use the word 'present'. He says 'everlasting life'—eternity: enter eternity.

Time we divide in three: past, present, future. That division is false, absolutely false. Time is really past and future. The present is not part of time; the present is part of eternity. That which

24

has passed is time, that which is to come is time. That which *is* is not time, because it never passes, it is always there. The now is always here—it is *always* here. This now is eternal.

If you move from the past, you never move in the present. From the past you always move into the future. There comes no moment which is present. From the past you *always* move into the future. From the present you can never move into the future. From the present you go deep and deep. . .and more present and more present. . . that is everlasting life.

We may say it in this way: from past to future is time. Time means you move on the plane, in a straight line, or we may say it is horizontal. The moment you are in the present, the dimension changes. You move vertically—up or down, towards the height or towards the depth. But then you never move horizontally. A Buddha, a Shiva, lives in eternity not in time.

Jesus was asked: "What will happen in your Kingdom of God?" The man who asked him was not asking about time. He was asking about what is going to happen to his desires: "How will they be fulfilled? Will there be life everlasting or will there be death? Will there be any misery? Will

ferior and superior men?" He was ask-
_____ of this world: "What is going to happen
in your Kingdom of God?"

And Jesus replied—the reply is like a Zen monk
—Jesus said: "There shall be time no longer." He
may not have understood at all, the man who was
answered this way: "There shall be time no
longer." Only one thing Jesus said: "There shall
be time no longer"— because time is horizontal
and the Kingdom of God is vertical; it is eternal. It
is always here; only *you* have to move away from
time to enter in it.

So love is the first door. . .you can move away
from time. That's why everyone wants to be
loved, everyone wants to love. And no one knows
why so much significance for love is there, why
such deep longing for love. And unless you know
it rightly you can neither love nor be loved, because love is one of the deepest phenomena upon
this earth.

We go on thinking that everyone is capable of
love as he is. This is not the case; it is not so.
That's why you are frustrated. Love is a different
dimension. And if you try to love someone *in*
time, you will be defeated in your effort. In time,
love is not possible.

I remember one anecdote:

Meera was in love with Krishna. She was a housewife—the wife of a prince. The prince became jealous of Krishna. Krishna was no more, Krishna was not present; Krishna was not a physical body. There is a gap of five thousand years between Krishna's physical existence and Meera's physical existence. So, really, how can Meera be in love with Krishna? The time gap is so great!

So one day the prince asked Meera, her husband asked her, "You go on talking about your love, you go on dancing and singing around Krishna, but where is he? With whom are you so much in love? With whom are you talking continuously?" Meera was talking with Krishna, singing, laughing, fighting. She looked mad! She was, in our eyes. So the prince said, "Have you gone mad? Where is your Krishna? Whom are you loving? With whom are you conversing? And I am here and you have completely forgotten me."

Meera said, "Krishna is here, you are not here, because Krishna is eternal, you are not. He will be always here, he was always here, he is here. You will not be here, you were not here. You were not here one day, you will not be here. . .so how can I believe that between these two non-existences you are here? How is existence possible between two non-existences?"

The prince is in time, Krishna is in eternity. So you can be near the prince, but the distance cannot be destroyed. You will be distant. You may be very, very distant in time from Krishna, still you can be near. But it is a different dimension.

I look in front of me and there is a wall. I move my eyes and there is sky. When you look in time, there is always a wall. When you look beyond time, there is open sky, infinite. Love opens the infinity, the everlastingness of existence. So, really, if you have ever loved, love can be made a technique of meditation. This is the technique:

> *While being* loved, *sweet princess, enter* the loving *as everlasting life.*

Don't be a lover standing aloof, out. Become loving and move into eternity. When you are loving someone, are you there as the lover? If you are there you are in time and love is just false, just pseudo. If you are still there and you can say, "I am," then you can be physically near but spiritually you are poles apart.

While in love, you must not be—only love, only

loving. Become loving! Caressing your beloved or your lover, become the caress. Kissing, don't be the kisser or the kissed, be the kiss. Forget the ego completely; dissolve it into the act. Move into the act so deeply that the actor is no more. And if you cannot move in love, it is difficult to move in eating or walking—very difficult, because love is the easiest approach to dissolve the ego. That's why those who are egoists, they cannot love. They may talk about it, they may sing about it, they may write about it, but they cannot love. The ego cannot love.

Shiva says become loving. When you are in the embrace, become the embrace, become the kiss. Forget yourself so totally that you can say, "I am no more. Only love exists." Then the heart is not beating, but love is beating. Then the blood is not circulating, love is circulating. Then eyes are not seeing, love is seeing. Then hands are not moving to touch, love is moving to touch.

Become love!—and enter everlasting life. Love suddenly changes your dimension. You are thrown out of time and you are facing eternity.

Love can become a deep meditation, the deepest possible. And lovers have known sometimes what saints have not known. Lovers have touched

that center which many yogis have missed. But it
will be just a glimpse unless you transform your
love into meditation. Tantra means this: transformation of love into meditation. And now you
can understand why Tantra talks so much about
love and sex. Why? Because love is the easiest
natural door from where you can transcend this
world, this horizontal dimension.

Look at Shiva with his consort Devi. Look at
them! They don't seem to be two; they are one.
The oneness is so deep that it has gone even into
symbols. We all have seen the Shivalinga. That is
a phallic symbol—Shiva's sex organ. But it is not
alone; it is based in Devi's vagina. The Hindus of
those days were very daring. Now when you see a
Shivalinga, you never remember it is a phallic
symbol. We have forgotten; we have tried to
forget it completely.

Jung remembers in his autobiography, in his
memoirs, a very beautiful and funny incident. He
came to India, he went to see Konarak, and in the
temple of Konarak there are many, many Shivalingas, many phallic symbols. The pundit who
was taking him around explained everything to
him except Shivalingas. And they were so many it
was difficult to escape. Jung was well aware, but

just to tease the pundit he went on asking, "But what are these?" So the pundit at last said in his ear, in Jung's ear, "Don't ask me here. I will tell you afterwards. This is a private thing." Jung must have laughed inside. These are the Hindus of today.

Then outside the temple the pundit came near and he said, "It was not good of you to ask before others. I will tell you now. It is a secret." And then again in Jung's ear he said, "They are our private parts."

When Jung went back, he met one great scholar —a scholar of oriental thought, myth, philosophy —Heinrich Zimmer. So he related this anecdote to Zimmer. Zimmer was one of the most gifted minds who tried to penetrate Indian thought, and he was a lover of India and its ways of thinking— the oriental, non-logical, mystic approach towards life. When he heard this from Jung, he laughed and he said, "This is good for a change. I have always heard about *great* Indians—Buddha, Krishna, Mahavira. What you relate tells not about any great Indian, but about Indians."

Love, for Shiva, is the great gate. And for him sex is also not something to be condemned. For him sex is the seed and love is the flowering of it.

And if you condemn the seed, you condemn the flower. Sex can become love. If it never becomes love, then it is crippled. Condemn the crippledness, not the sex. Love must flower; sex must become love. If it is not becoming, it is not the fault of sex. It is your fault.

Sex must not remain sex—that is the Tantra teaching—it must be transformed into love. And love also must not remain love. It must be transformed into light, into meditative experience, into the last, ultimate, mystic peak. How to transform love? Be the act and forget the actor. While loving, be love—simple love. Then it is not your love or my love or anybody else's. It is simple love. When you are not there, then you are in the hands of an ultimate source, current, then you are in love. It is not *you* who is in love; then the love has engulfed you, you have disappeared. You have become just a flowing energy.

D.H. Lawrence, one of the most creative minds of this age, was, knowingly or unknowingly, a Tantra adept. He was condemned in the West completely; his books were banned. There were many cases in the courts—because he said that sex energy is the only energy, and if you condemn it and suppress it you are against the universe and you will never be capable of knowing the higher flowering of this energy.

And when suppressed it becomes ugly. This is the vicious circle: priests, moralists, so-called religious people, popes, *shankaracharyas* and others, they go on condemning sex. They say this is an ugly thing. When you suppress it, it becomes ugly, so they say: "Look! What we said is true. It is proved by you. Look! Whatsoever you are doing is ugly and you know it is ugly."

But it is not sex which is ugly, it is these priests who have made it ugly. And once they have made it ugly, they are proved right. And when they are proved right, you go on making it more and more ugly—uglier.

Sex is innocent energy, life flowing in you, existence alive in you. Don't cripple it. Allow it to move towards heights—that is, sex must become love. What is the difference? When your mind is sexual you are exploiting the other. The other is just an instrument to be used and thrown. When sex becomes love, the other is not an instrument, the other is not to be exploited. The other is not really the other. When you love, it is not self-centered. Rather, the other becomes significant, unique.

It is not that you are exploiting him—no. On the contrary, you both are joining in a deep experience. You are partners of a deep experience, not the exploiter and the exploited. You are helping each other to move in a different world, of love. Sex is exploitation. Love is moving together into a different world.

If this moving is not momentary, and if this moving becomes meditative, that is if you can forget yourself completely and the lover and the beloved disappear and there is only love flowing, then, Shiva says, everlasting life is yours.

Total Let-go in Sex

*"Sex transferred to the head
is sexuality."*

Whatsoever you do, do it meditatively
and totally—even sex. It is easy to conceive how to be angry alone, but you
can also create a sexual orgy alone meditatively.
And you will have a different quality after that.

While all alone, just close your room and move
as if in the sex act. Allow your whole body to
move. Jump and scream—do whatsoever you feel
like doing. Do it totally. Forget everything—society, inhibitions, etc. Move in the sex act alone,
meditatively, but bring your total sexuality to it.

With the other, the society is always present
because the other is present. And it is so difficult
to be in such a deep love that you can feel as if the
other is not present. Only in a very deep love, in a

very deep intimacy, is it possible to be with your lover or beloved as if he is not or she is not.

This is what intimacy means: if you are as if alone with your lover or beloved or your spouse in the room, with no fear of the other, then you can move in the sex act totally. Otherwise the other is always an inhibiting presence. The other is looking at you: "What will she think? What will he think? What are you doing? Behaving like an animal?"

One lady was here just a few days before. She came to complain against her husband. She said, "I cannot tolerate it. Whenever he loves me, he starts behaving like an animal."

When the other is present, the other is looking at you: "What are you doing?" And you have been taught not to do some things. It inhibits; you cannot move totally.

If love is really there, then you can move as if you are alone. And when two bodies become one, they have a single rhythm. Then the two-ness is lost, and sex can be released totally. And it is not like in anger.

Anger is always ugly; sex is not always ugly. Sometimes it is the most beautiful thing possible, but only sometimes. When the meeting is perfect, when the two become one rhythm, when their breaths have become one and their *prana* flows in a circle, when the two have disappeared completely and the two bodies have become one whole, when the negative and positive, the male and female, are no more there, then sex is the most beautiful thing possible. But that is not always the case.

If it is not possible, you can bring your sex act to a climax of frenzy and madness while alone, in a meditative mood. Close the room, meditate in it, and allow your body to move as if you are not controlling it. Lose all control!

Spouses can be very helpful, and particularly in Tantra: your wife, your husband, or your friend can be very helpful if you both are experimenting deeply. Then allow each total uncontrol. Forget civilization as if it never existed. Move back into the Garden of Eden. Throw that apple—the fruit of the Tree of Knowledge. Be Adam and Eve in the Garden of Eden before they were expelled. Move back! Just be like innocent animals and act out your sexuality in its totality. You will never be the same again.

Two things will happen. Sexuality will disappear; sex may remain, but sexuality will disappear completely. And when there is no sexuality, sex is divine. When the cerebral hankering is not there, when you are not thinking about it, when it has become a simple involvement—a total act, a movement of your whole being, not only of the mind—it is divine. Sexuality will disappear first, and then sex may also disappear, because once you know the deeper core of it you can achieve that core without sex.

But you have not known that deeper core, so how can you achieve it? The first glimpse comes through total sex. Once known, the path can be traveled in other ways also. Just looking at a flower, you can be in the same ecstasy in which you are when you meet with your spouse in a climax. Just watching the stars, you can move in it.

Once you know the path, you know it is within you. The spouse only helps you to know it, and you help your spouse to know it. It is within you! The other was just a provocation, the other was just a challenge, to help you know something which was always within you.

And this is what is happening between a Master and a disciple. The Master can become only a challenge to you to show that which has always been hidden in you. The Master is not giving you anything. He cannot give; there is nothing to give. And all that can be given is worthless because it will be only a thing.

That which cannot be given but only provoked is worthwhile. A Master is just provoking you. He challenges you to help you to come to a point where you can realize something which is already there. Once you know it, there is no need of a Master.

Sex may disappear, but first disappears sexuality. Then sex becomes a pure, innocent act; then sex also disappears. Then there is *brahmacharya*. It is not opposite to sex, it is just its absence. And remember this difference; this is not in your awareness.

Old religions go on condemning anger and sex as if both are the same or as if both belong to the same category. They do not! Anger is destructive, sex is creative. All old religions go on condemning them in a similar way, as if anger and sex, greed and sex, jealousy and sex, are similar. They are not! Jealousy is destructive—always! It is never creative; nothing can come out of it. Anger is always destructive, but not so with sex!

Sex is the source of creativity. The divine has

used it for creation. Sexuality is just like jealousy, anger and greed—it is always destructive. Sex is not, but we don't know pure sex. We know only sexuality.

A person who is looking at a pornographic picture or one who is going to see a film, a movie of sexual orgies, is not seeking sex: he is seeking sexuality. There are persons whom I know who cannot make love to their wives unless they first go through some dirty magazines or books or pictures. When they see these pictures then they are excited. The real wife is nothing to them. A picture, a nude picture, is more exciting to them. That excitement is not in the gut; that excitement is in the mind, in the head.

Sex transferred to the head is sexuality; thinking about it is sexuality. Living it is a different thing, and if you can live it you can go beyond it. Anything lived totally leads you beyond. So don't be afraid of anything. Live it!

If you think it is destructive to others, move in it alone; don't do it with others. If you think it is creative, then find a partner, find a friend. Become a couple, a Tantric couple, and move in it totally. If you still feel that the other's presence is inhibiting, then you can do it alone.

The Spirituality of the Tantric Sex Act

"The other is simply a door.
While making love to a woman,
you are really making love
to Existence itself."

SIGMUND FREUD says somewhere that man is born neurotic. This is a half-truth. Man is not born neurotic but born in a neurotic humanity, and the society around drives everyone neurotic sooner or later. Man is born natural, real, normal. But the moment the newborn becomes part of the society, neurosis starts working.

As we are, we are neurotic. And the neurosis consists of a split—a deep split. You are not one; you are two or even many. This has to be understood deeply; only then can we proceed in Tantra. Your feeling and thinking have become two different things; this is the basic neurosis. Your thinking part and your feeling part have become two, and you are identified with the thinking part, not with the feeling part. And feeling is more real than thinking; feeling is more natural than thinking. You have come with a feeling heart, the thinking is cultivated; it is given by society. And your feeling has become a suppressed thing. Even when you say you feel, you only think that you feel. The feeling has become dead. And it has happened for certain reasons.

When a child is born, he is a feeling being. He feels things; he is not a thinking being yet. He is natural, just like anything natural in nature—just like a tree or like an animal. But we start molding him, cultivating. He has to suppress his feelings, because without suppressing his feelings he is always in trouble. When he wants to cry he cannot cry because his parents will not approve of it. He will be condemned, he will not be appreciated, he will not be loved. He is not accepted as he is. He must behave. He must behave according to a particular ideology, ideals; only then will he be loved.

Love is not for him as he is. He can be loved only if he follows certain rules. Those rules are imposed; they are not natural. The natural being starts being suppressed, and the unnatural, the unreal, is imposed over it. This unreal is your mind, and a moment comes when the split is so great that you cannot bridge it. You go on forgetting completely what your real nature was—or is. You are a false face; the original face is lost. And you are afraid also to feel the original, because the moment you feel it the whole society will be against you. So you yourself are against your real nature.

This creates a very neurotic state. You don't know what you want; you don't know what are your real, authentic needs. And then one goes on for non-authentic needs, because only the feeling heart can give you the sense, the direction. . . what is your real need? When it is suppressed, you create symbolic needs. For example, you may go on eating more and more, stuffing yourself with food, and you can never feel that you are filled. The need is for love, it is not for food, but food and love are deeply related. So when the love need is not felt or is suppressed, a false need for food is created. And you can go on eating. Because the need is false, it can never be fulfilled. And we live in false needs; that's why there is no fulfillment.

You want to be loved; that's a basic need, natural, but it can be diverted into a false dimension. For example, the love need, being loved, can be felt as a false need if you try to divert others' attention to yourself. You want that others should pay attention to you. You may become a political leader—great crowds paying attention to you—but the real basic need is to be loved, and even if the whole world is paying attention to you, that basic need cannot be fulfilled. That basic need can even be fulfilled by a single person loving you, paying attention to you, because of love.

When you love someone you pay attention. Attention and love are deeply related. If you suppress the love need, then it becomes a symbolic need—you need others' attention. You may get it, but then too there will be no fulfillment. The need is false, disconnected from the natural, basic need. This division in the personality is neurosis.

Tantra is a very revolutionary concept—the oldest and yet the newest. Tantra is one of the oldest traditions and yet non-traditional, even anti-traditional, because Tantra says unless you are whole and one, you are missing life altogether. You should not remain in a split state; you must become one.

44

What to do to become one? You can go on thinking; that is not going to help because thinking is the technique to divide. Thinking is analytical. It divides, splits things. Feeling unites, synthesizes, makes things one. So you can go on thinking, reading, studying, contemplating. It is not going to help, unless you fall back to the feeling center. But it is very difficult because even when we think about the feeling center, we think!

When you say to someone, "I love you," be aware of whether it is just a thought or a feeling. If it is just a thought, then you are missing something. A feeling is of the whole; your whole body, mind, everything you are, is involved. In thinking only your head is involved, and that too not totally—just a fragment of it, a passing thought. It may not be there the next moment. Only a fragment is involved, and that creates much misery in life, because for a fragmentary thought you can give promises which you cannot fulfill. You can say, "I love you and I will love you forever." Now the second part is a promise which you cannot fulfill because it is given by a fragmentary thought. Your whole being is not involved in it. And what will you do tomorrow when the fragment has gone and the thought is no more there? Now the promise will become a bondage.

Sartre says somewhere that every promise is going to be false. You cannot promise because you are not whole! Just a part of me promises, and when the part is no more there on the throne, another part has taken over, what am I going to do? Who will fulfill the promise? Hypocrisy is born because then I go on trying to fulfill, I pretend that I am fulfilling. . .then everything becomes false.

Tantra says fall down deep within to the feeling center. What to do and how to fall back? Now I will enter the sutras. These sutras, each sutra, is an effort to make you whole.

The first:

> *At the start of sexual union, keep attentive on the fire in the beginning, and, so continuing, avoid the embers in the end.*

Sex can be a very deep fulfillment and sex can throw you back to your wholeness, to your natural, real being, for many reasons. Those reasons have to be understood. One, sex is a total act. You are thrown off your mind, off balance. That's why there is so much fear of sex. You are identified with the mind and sex is a no-mind act. You become headless. You don't have any head in the act. There is no reasoning, no mental process. And if there is mental process, there is no real, authentic sex act. Then there is no orgasm, no fulfillment. Then the sex act itself becomes a local thing, something cerebral, and it has become so.

All over the world, so much hankering, so much lust for sex, is not because the world has become more sexual. It is because you cannot even enjoy sex as a total act. The world was more sexual before. That's why there was no such hankering for sex. This hankering shows that the real is missing and we are for the false. The whole modern mind has become sexual because the sex act itself is no more there. Even the sex act is transferred to the mind; it has become mental. You *think* about it.

Many people come to me: they say they go on thinking about sex; they enjoy thinking about it —reading, seeing pictures, pornography, they enjoy. But when the actual moment for sex comes they suddenly feel they are not interested. They even feel they have become impotent. They feel vital energy when they are thinking. When they want to move into the actual act, they feel there is no energy, even no desire. They feel their body has become dead.

What is happening to them? Even the sex act has become mental. They can only think about it; they cannot do it because doing will involve their whole being. And whenever there is any involvement of the whole, the head becomes uneasy—because then it can no more be the master, it can no more be in control.

Tantra uses the sex act to make you whole, but then you have to move in it very meditatively. Then you have to move in it forgetting all that you have heard about sex, studied about sex, the society has told you, the church, the religion, the teachers. . .forget everything, and get involved in it in your totality. Forget to control! Control is the barrier. Rather, be possessed by it; don't control it.

Move in it as if you have become mad—no-mind looks like madness. Become the body, become the animal, because the animal is whole. And as modern man is, only sex seems to be the easiest possibility to make you whole, because sex is the deepest, the biological center within you. You are born out of it. Your each cell is a sex cell. Your whole body is a sex-energy phenomenon.

This first sutra says:

> *At the start of sexual union keep attentive on the fire in the beginning, and, so continuing, avoid the embers in the end.*

And this makes the whole difference. For you, the sexual act is a release. So when you move in it you are in a hurry. You just want a release. Overflowing energy will be released; you will feel at ease. This at-easeness is just a sort of weakness. Overflowing energy creates tensions, excitement. You feel something has to be done. When the energy is released, you feel weak. You may take this weakness as relaxation, because the excitement is no more, the overflowing energy is no more. You *can* relax! But this relaxation is a negative relaxation. If you can relax just by throwing energy, it is at a very great cost. And this relaxation can be only physical. It cannot go deeper and cannot become spiritual.

This first sutra says don't be in a hurry and don't hanker for the end. Remain with the beginning. There are two parts in the sexual act: the beginning and the end. Remain with the beginning. The beginning part is more relaxed, warm. But don't be in a hurry to move to the end. Forget the end completely.

> *At the start of sexual union, keep attention on the fire in the beginning. . .*

While you are overflowing, don't think in terms of release. Remain with this overflowing energy. Don't seek ejaculation. Forget it completely! Be whole in this warm beginning. Remain with your beloved or your lover as if you have become one. Create a circle.

There are three possibilities. Two lovers meeting can create three figures—geometrical figures. You may have even read about it or even seen one old alchemical picture in which a man and woman are standing naked within three geometrical figures. One figure is a square, another figure is a triangle, and the third figure is a circle.

This is one of the old alchemical and Tantric analyses of the sexual act. Ordinarily, when you are in the sexual act there are four persons, not two—this is a square. Four angles are there: because you yourself are divided in two—the thinking part and the feeling part—your partner is also divided in two. You are four persons. Two persons are not meeting there, four persons are meeting. It is a crowd. And there can be no deep meeting really. There are four corners, and the meeting is just false. It looks like a meeting, it is not. There can be no communion, because your deeper part is hidden and your beloved's deeper part is also hidden. And only two heads are meeting, only two thinking processes are meeting, not two feeling processes. They are hidden.

The second type of meeting can be like a triangle. You are two—two angles of the base. For a sudden moment you become one, like the third angle of the triangle. But for a sudden moment. . . your twoness is lost and you become one. This is better than the square meeting, because at least for a single moment there is oneness. That oneness gives you health, vitality. You feel again alive and young.

But the third is the best, and the third is the Tantra meeting: you become a circle. There are no angles, and the meeting is not for a single moment. The meeting is really non-temporal; there is no time in it. And this can happen only if you are not seeking ejaculation. If you are seeking ejaculation, then it will become a triangle meeting —because the moment there is ejaculation the contact point is lost.

Remain with the beginning; don't move to the end. How to remain in the beginning? Many things to be remembered.

First, don't take the sex act as going anywhere. Don't take it as a means—it is the end in itself. There is no end to it; it is not a means. Secondly, don't think of the future; remain with the present. And if you cannot remain in the present in the beginning part of a sexual act, then you can never remain in the present—because the very nature of the act is such that you are thrown to the present.

Remain in the present. Enjoy the meeting of two bodies, two souls, and merge into each other . . .melt into each other. Forget that you are going anywhere. Remain in the moment going no-where, and melt. Warmth, love, should be made a situation to melt into each other.

That's why, if there is no love, the sex act is a hurried act. You are using the other; the other is just a means. And the other is using you. You are exploiting each other, not merging into each other. With love you can merge. This merging, in the beginning, will give many new insights.

If you are not in a hurry to finish the act, the act by and by becomes less and less sexual and more and more spiritual. Sex organs also melt into each other. A deep, silent communion happens between two body energies, and then you can remain for hours together. This togetherness moves deeper and deeper as time passes. But don't think. Remain with the moment, deeply merged. It becomes an ecstasy, a samadhi. And if you can know this, if you can feel and realize this, your sexual mind will become non-sexual. A very deep *brahmacharya* can be attained, celibacy can be attained through it.

This looks paradoxical because we have been thinking always in terms that if a person has to remain celibate, he must not look at the other sex, must not meet. . .avoid, escape! A very false celibacy happens then: the mind goes on thinking about the other sex. And the more you escape from the other, the more you have to think, because it is a basic, deep need.

Tantra says don't try to escape—there is no escape possible. Rather, use nature itself to transcend. Don't fight! Accept nature in order to transcend it. This communion with your beloved or your lover, if prolonged, with no end, just remaining in the beginning. . . Excitement is energy. You can lose it, you can come to a peak, and then the energy is lost and a depression will follow, a weakness will follow. You may take it as relaxation—it is negative.

Tantra gives you a dimension of a higher relaxation which is positive. Both the partners meet into each other, give vital energy to each other; they become a circle, and their energy begins to move in a circle. They are giving life to each other, renewing life. No energy is lost. Rather, more energy is gained, because through the contact with the opposite sex your every cell is challenged, excited. And if you can merge in that excitement not leading it to a peak, remaining in the beginning, not getting hot, remaining warm, those two warmths will meet.

You can prolong the act for a very long time. Without ejaculation, without throwing energy out, it becomes a meditation. And through it you become whole. Through it your split personality is no more split—it is bridged.

All neurosis is splitness. If you are bridged again, you have become again a child, innocent. And once you know this innocence you can go on behaving in your society as it requires, but now this behavior is just a drama, acting. You are not involved in it. It is a requirement—you do it, you are not in it. You are just acting. You will have to use unreal faces, you live in an unreal world; otherwise, the world will crush you and kill you.

We have killed many real faces. We crucified

Jesus because he started behaving like a real man. The unreal society will not tolerate it. We poisoned Socrates because he started behaving like a real man.

Behave as the society requires; don't create unnecessary troubles for yourself and others. But once you know your real being and the wholeness, the unreal society cannot drive you neurotic; it cannot make you mad.

> *At the start of sexual union, keep attentive on the fire in the beginning, and, so continuing, avoid the embers in the end.*

If ejaculation is there, energy is dissipated. Then there is no more fire. You are simply relieved of your energy without gaining anything.

The second sutra:

> *When in such embrace your senses are shaken as leaves, enter this shaking.*

While *in such embrace*—in such deep communion with the beloved or the lover— *your senses are shaken as leaves, enter this shaking.*

We have even become afraid. . .while making

love, we don't allow our bodies to move much—because if your bodies are allowed to move much the sex act spreads all over your body. You can control it when it is localized at the sex center; the mind can remain in control. When it spreads all over your body, you cannot control it. You may start shaking, you may start screaming, and you will not be able to control your body once the body takes over.

We suppress movements. Particularly, all over the world, we suppressed all movements, all shaking, of women. They remain just like dead bodies. You are doing something to them; they are not doing anything to you. They are just passive partners. Why did this happen? Why all over the world did men suppress women in such a way?

There is fear—because once a woman's body becomes possessed, it is very difficult for a man to satisfy her: because a woman can have chain orgasms; a man cannot have. A man can have only one orgasm; a woman can have chain orgasms. There are cases of multiple orgasms reported. Any woman can have at least three orgasms in a chain, but man can have only one. And with man's orgasm, the woman is aroused and is ready for further orgasm. Then it is difficult. Then how to manage it?

She needs another man immediately, and group sex is taboo. All over the world we have created monogamous societies. So it is better to suppress the woman. So, really, eighty percent to ninety percent of women never know what orgasm is. They can give birth to children; that's another thing. They can satisfy the man; that's also another thing. But they themselves are never satisfied. So if you see such bitterness in women all over the world—sadness, bitterness, frustration—it is natural. Their basic need is not fulfilled.

Shaking is just wonderful because when you shake in your sexual act, the energy starts flowing all over the body, the energy vibrates all over the body. Every cell of the body is involved then. Every cell becomes alive, because every cell is a sex cell.

When you were born, two sex cells met and your being was created, your body was created. Those two sex cells are everywhere in your body. They have multiplied and multiplied, and multiplied, but your basic unit remains the sex cell. When you shake all over your body, it is not only a meeting of you with your beloved; within your body also, each cell is meeting with the opposite cell. This shaking shows it. It will look animal-like, but man *is* an animal and there is nothing wrong in it.

This second sutra says:

> *When in such embrace your senses are shaken as leaves. . .*

A great wind is blowing and the tree is shaking, even the roots are shaken, every leaf is shaking. Just be like a tree! A great wind is blowing, and sex *is* a great wind—a great energy blowing through you. Shake! Vibrate! Allow your every cell of the body to dance. And this should be for both. The beloved is also dancing, every cell vibrating. Only then can you both meet. And then that meeting is not mental—it is a meeting of your bio-energies.

Enter this shaking, and while shaking don't remain aloof, don't be a spectator, because mind is the spectator. Don't stand aloof! *Be* the shaking, *become* the shaking. Forget everything and become the shaking. It is not that your body is shaking: it is you, your whole being. You have become the shaking itself. Then there are not two bodies,

two minds. In the beginning two shaking energies
. . .and in the end just a circle, not two.

What will happen in this circle? One, you will
be part of an existential force—not a societal mind
but an existential force. You will be part of the
whole cosmos; in that shaking you will be part of
the whole cosmos. That moment is of great creation. You are dissolved as solid bodies. You have
become liquid, flowing into each other. The mind
is lost. The division is lost. You have a oneness.

This is *adwaita*—this is non-duality. And if you
cannot feel this non-duality, then all the philoso-
phies of non-duality are useless. They are just
words. Once you know this non-dual existential
moment, then only can you understand the Upan-
ishads, then only can you understand the mystics,
what they are talking about—a cosmic oneness, a
wholeness. Then you are not separate from the
world, not an alien to it. Then the existence becomes your home.

And with that feeling, that "Now I am at home
in existence," all worries are lost. Then there is
no anguish, no struggle, no conflict. Lao Tzu calls
this Tao, Shankara calls it *adwaita*. You can
choose your own word, but it is easy to feel
through a deep love embrace. But be alive, shaking, and become the shaking itself.

Third sutra:

*Even remembering union, without the embrace,
the transformation.*

Once you know it, even the partner is not
needed. You can simply remember the act and
enter into it. But you must have the feeling first. If
you know the feeling, you can enter into the act
without the partner. This is a little difficult, but it
happens. And unless it happens, you go on being
dependent—a dependency is created. For so
many reasons it happens.

If you have had the feeling, if you have known
the moment when you were not there but only a
vibrating energy in which you have become one
and there was a circle with the partner, in that
moment there is no partner. Only you are, and for
the partner you are not: only he or she is.

Because that oneness is centered within you,
the partner is no more there. And it is easier for
women to have this feeling because they are always making love with closed eyes.

During this technique, it is good if you have
your eyes closed. Then only an inner feeling of a
circle, only an inner feeling of oneness, is there.
Then just remember it. Close your eyes, lie down

as if you are with your partner, just remember, and start feeling it. Your body will begin to shake and vibrate.

Allow it. Forget completely that the other is not there. Move as if the other is. Only in the beginning is it 'as if'. Once you know it, it is not 'as if'; then the other is there. Move as if you are actually going into the love act. Do whatsoever you would have done with your partner. Scream, move, shake. Soon the circle will be there—and this circle is miraculous. Soon you will feel the circle is created. And now this circle is not created with a man and woman. If you are man, then the whole universe has become woman. If you are woman, then the whole universe has become man. Now you are in a deep communion with existence itself, and the door, the other, is no more there.

The other is simply a door. While making love to a woman, you are really making love to existence itself. The woman is just a door, the man is just a door. The other is just a door for the whole. But you are in such a hurry you never feel it. If you remain in communion, in deep embrace for hours together, you will forget the other and the other will just become an extension of the whole.

Once known, you can use this technique alone.

And when you can use it alone, it gives you a new freedom—freedom from the other. Really, it happens that the whole existence becomes the other —your beloved, your lover. And then this technique can be used continuously, and one can remain in constant communion with existence.

And you can do it then in other dimensions also. Walking in the morning, you can do it. Then you are in communion with the air, with the rising sun, and the sky and the trees. Staring at the stars in the night, you can do it. Looking at the moon, you can do it. You can be in the sex act with the whole universe once you know how it happens.

But it is good to start with human beings because they are nearest to you—the nearest part of the universe. But they are dispensable. You can take a jump and forget the door completely.

> *Even remembering union. . .the transformation.*

And you will be transformed, you will become new.

Tantra uses sex as a vehicle. It is energy; it can be used as a vehicle. It can transform you and it can give you transcendental states.

But as we are using sex it looks difficult for us, because we are using it in a very wrong way. And the wrong way is not natural; animals are better than us. They are using it in a natural way; our ways are perverted. Constant hammering on the human mind that sex is sin has created a deep barrier within you. You never allow yourself a total let-go. Something is always standing aloof, condemning. Even for the new generation. . .they may say they are not burdened, obsessed, that sex is not taboo for them, but you cannot unburden your unconscious so easily. It has been built for centuries and centuries. The whole human past is there. So while consciously you may not be condemning it as sin, the unconscious is there and constantly condemning it. You are never totally in it. Something is always left out. That left out part creates the split.

Tantra says move in it totally. Just forget yourself, your civilization, your religion, your culture, your ideology. Forget everything! Just move—move in it totally. Don't leave anything out. Become absolutely non-thinking. Only then the awareness happens that you have become one with someone.

And this feeling of oneness then can be detached from the partner and it can be used with the whole universe. You can be in a sex act with a tree, with the moon—with anything! Once you know how to create this circle, it can be created with anything—even without anything.

You can create this circle within you, because man is both man and woman, and woman is both man and woman. You are both because you were created by two; you were created by man and woman both, so half of you remains the other. You can forget everything completely, and the circle can be created within you. Once the circle is created within you—your man meeting your woman, the inner woman meeting the inner man —you are in an embrace within yourself. And only when this circle is created is real celibacy attained. Otherwise, all celibacies are just perversions, and they create their own problems.

This circle, when created inside, you are freed. This is what Tantra says: Sex is the deepest bondage, yet it can be used as a vehicle for the highest freedom. Tantra says poison can be used as medicine—wisdom is needed.

So don't condemn anything. Rather, use it. And don't be against anything. Find out ways how it can be used and transformed. Tantra is deep, total acceptance of life. The only approach. . .all over the world, in all the centuries that have gone by, Tantra is unique. It says: Don't throw anything and don't be against anything and don't create any conflict—because with any conflict you will be destructive with yourself.

All the religions are against sex, afraid of it, because it is such a great energy. Once you are in it you are no more, and then the current will take you anywhere; that's why the fear. So: "Create a barrier so that you and the current become two! And don't allow this vital energy to have any possession over you—be master of it!"

Only Tantra says this mastery is going to be false, diseased, pathological, because you cannot really be divided from this current. You are it! So all divisions will be false, arbitrary. And, basically, no division is possible, because you are the current—part and parcel of it, just a wave in it. You can get frozen and separate yourself from the current, but that frozenness will be deadness. And humanity has become dead. No one is really alive—just dead weights floating in the stream. Melt! Tantra says try to melt. Don't become like icebergs: melt and become one with the river.

Becoming one with the river, feeling one with

the river, merging in the river, be aware, and there will be transformation—there *is* transformation. Transformation is not through conflict, it is through awareness.

These three techniques are very, very scientific, but then sex becomes something other than what you know. Then it is not a temporary relief. Then it is not throwing energy out. Then there is no end to it. It becomes a meditative circle.

A few more related techniques:

> *On joyously seeing a long-absent friend, permeate this joy.*

Enter this joy and become one with it—any joy, any happiness. This is just an example:

> *On joyously seeing a long-absent friend. . .*

Suddenly you see a friend you have not seen for many, many days or many, many years. A sudden joy grips you. But your attention will be on the friend, not on your joy; then you are missing something. And this joy is momentary, and your attention is focused on the friend. You will start talking, remembering things, and you will miss this joy and this joy will go.

When you see a friend and suddenly feel a joy

arising in your heart, concentrate on this joy. Feel it and become it. And meet the friend being aware and filled with your joy. Let the friend be just on the periphery and you remain centered in your feeling of happiness.

This can be done in many other situations. The sun is rising, and suddenly you feel something rising within you. Then forget the sun; let it remain on the periphery. You be centered in your own feeling of rising energy. The moment you look at it, it will spread. It will become your whole body, your whole being. And don't just be an observer of it—merge into it! There are very few moments when you feel joy, happiness, bliss. But we go on missing them because we become object centered.

Whenever there is joy, you feel it is coming from without. You have seen a friend; of course, it appears that the joy is coming from your friend, seeing him. That is not the actual case. The joy is always within you. The friend has just become a situation; the friend has helped it to come out, but it is there. And this is not only with joy, but with everything: with anger, with sadness, with misery, with happiness—with everything it is so. Others are only situations in which things which are hidden within you are expressed. They are not causes; they are not causing something in you. Whatsoever is happening is happening to you. It has always been there; only this meeting with a friend has become a situation in which whatsoever was hidden has come open, has come out. From the hidden sources, it has become apparent, manifest.

Whenever this happens, remain centered in the inner feeling. And then your life will have a different attitude about everything. Even with negative emotions, do it.

When you are angry, don't be centered on the person who has aroused it. Let him be on the periphery. You just become anger, you feel it in its totality—allow it to happen within. Don't rationalize; don't say, "This man has created it." Don't condemn the man. He has become just a situation. And feel grateful towards him, that something that was hidden has become open. He has hit somewhere, and a wound was there hidden. Now you know it—become the wound.

With negative or positive, any emotions, use this, and there will be a great change in you. If the emotion is negative, you will be freed of it by being aware that it is within you; if the emotion is positive, you will become the emotion itself. If it is joy, you will become joy. If it is anger, the anger will dissolve.

And this is the difference between negative and positive emotions. If you become aware of a certain emotion, and the emotion by becoming aware dissolves, it is negative. If by becoming aware of a certain emotion, *you* become the emotion, and the emotion spreads and becomes your being, it is positive.

Awareness works differently on both. If it is poisonous, you are relieved of it through awareness. If it is good, blissful, ecstatic, you become one with it; awareness deepens it.

So, to me, this is the criterion: if something is deepened by your awareness, it is good; if something is dissolved through awareness, it is bad. That which cannot remain in awareness is sin, and that which grows in awareness is virtue. Virtue and sin are not social concepts; they are inner realizations.

Use your awareness. It is just like: if there is darkness and you bring light, the darkness will be no more there. Just by bringing light in, the darkness is no more there—because, really, it was not. It was negative, just the absence of light. But many things will become manifest which are there. Just by bringing light, these shelves, these books, these walls, will not disappear. In darkness they were not; you couldn't see them. If you bring light in, darkness will be no more there, but that which is real will be revealed.

Through awareness all that is negative like darkness will dissolve—hatred, anger, sadness, violence. Love, joy, ecstasy, they will, for the first time, become revealed to you.

> *On joyously seeing a long-absent friend, permeate this joy.*

The fifth technique:

> *When eating or drinking, become the taste of the food or drink, and be filled.*

We go on eating things, we cannot live without them, but we eat them very unconsciously, automatically, robotlike. The taste is not lived; you are just stuffing. Go slow, and be aware of the taste. And only when you go slow can you be aware. Don't just go on swallowing things. Taste them, unhurriedly, and become the taste. When you feel sweetness, become that sweetness. And then it can be felt all over the body—not just the mouth, not just the tongue. It can be felt all over the body! A certain sweetness spreading in ripples. . .or anything else! Whatsoever you are eating, feel the taste and become the taste. This is how Tantra looks quite the contrary from other traditions.

Jainas say, "No taste—*aswad*." Mahatma Gandhi had it as a rule in his ashram: "*Aswad*—don't taste anything. Eat, but don't taste; forget the taste. Eating is a necessity; do it in a mechanical way. Taste is desire, so don't taste." Tantra says taste it as much as possible; be more sensitive, alive. And not only sensitive—become the taste.

With *aswad*, with no taste, your senses will be deadened. They will become less and less sensitive. And with their lessened sensitivity you will not be able to feel your body, you will not be able to feel your feelings. Then you will just remain centered in the head. This centeredness in the head is the split. Tantra says don't create any division within yourself. It is beautiful to taste, it is beautiful to be sensitive. And the more sensitive you are, the more alive you will be, and the more alive you are, the more life will enter your inner being. You will be more open.

You can eat things without tasting; it is not

difficult. You can touch someone without touching; it is not difficult. We are already doing it. You shake hands with someone without touching him —because to touch, you have to come to the hand, move to the hand. You have to become your fingers and your palm—as if you, your soul, has come to the hand. Only then can you touch. You can take someone's hand in your hand and withdraw. You can withdraw; then the dead hand is there. It appears to be touching, but it is not touching.

We are not touching! We are afraid to touch somebody because touch has become symbolically sexual. You may be standing in a crowd, in a train, in a railway compartment, touching many persons, but you are not touching them and they are not touching you. Only bodies are there in contact, but you are withdrawn. And you can feel the difference: if you really touch someone in the crowd, he will feel offended. Your body can touch, but you must not move in that body. You must remain aloof, as if not in the body, only a dead body touching.

This insensitivity is bad. It is bad because you are defending yourself against life. We are so much afraid of death, and we are already dead.

We need not be afraid really, because no one is going to die—you are already dead! And that's why we are afraid, because we have not lived. We have been missing life, and death is coming.

A person who is alive will not be afraid of death, because he is living! While you are living really, there is no fear of death. You can even live death. When death comes, you will be so sensitive to it you will enjoy it. It is going to be a great experience. If you are alive you can live even death, and then death is no more there. If you can even live death, if you can even be sensitive to your dying body, and you are withdrawing to the center and dissolving, if you can live even this you have become deathless.

> *When eating or drinking, become the taste of the food or drink, and be filled. . .and be filled by the taste.*

Drinking water, feel the coolness. Close your eyes. . .drink slowly. . .taste it. Feel the coolness, and feel that *you* have become that coolness— because the coolness is being transferred to you from the water. It is becoming part of your body. Your mouth is touching, your tongue is touching, and the coolness is transferred. Allow it to happen to the whole of your body. Allow its ripples to spread, and *you* will feel a coolness all over your body. In this way your sensitivity can grow, and you can become more alive and more filled.

We are frustrated, feeling vacant, empty, and go on saying that life is empty. But we are the reason why it is empty. We are not filling it and we are not allowing anything to fill it. We have an armor around us, a defense armor, afraid to be vulnerable, so we go on defending against everything. And then we become a tomb—a dead thing.

Tantra says: Be alive, more alive, because *life is God*. There is no other God than life. Be more alive and you will be more divine. Be totally alive and there is no death for you.

Cosmic Orgasm
through Tantra

*"Sex is just the beginning,
not the end. But if you miss
the beginning,
you will miss the end also."*

BEFORE I TAKE YOUR QUESTIONS some other points have to be clarified, because those points will help you to understand more what Tantra means. Tantra is not a moral concept. It is neither moral nor immoral—it is amoral. It is a science; science is neither. Your moralities and concepts concerning moral behavior are irrelevant for Tantra. Tantra is not concerned with how one should behave. It is not concerned with ideals. It is concerned basically with what is, what you are. This distinction has to be understood deeply.

Morality is concerned with ideals—how you

should be, what you should be. Therefore, morality is basically condemning. You are never the ideal, so you are condemned. Every morality is guilt-creating. You can never become the ideal; you are always lagging behind. The gap will always be there because the ideal is the impossible. And through morality it becomes more impossible. The ideal is there in the future and you are here what you are, and you go on comparing. You are never the perfect man; something is lacking. You feel guilt, you feel a self-condemnation.

One thing: Tantra is against condemnation because condemnation can never transform you. Condemnation can only create hypocrisy. So what you are not, you try, you pretend to show. Hypocrisy means you are the real man, not the ideal man, but you pretend to show that you are the ideal man. Then you have a split within you, you have a false face. The unreal man is born, and Tantra is basically a search for the real man, not for the unreal man.

Every morality creates hypocrisy, of necessity. It will be so. Hypocrisy will remain with morality. It is part of it—the shadow. This will look paradoxical because moralists are the men who condemn hypocrisy most, and they are the creators of it. And hypocrisy cannot disappear from earth unless morality disappears. They both will exist together; they are aspects of the same coin. Because morality gives you the ideal and you are not the ideal; that's why the ideal is given to you. You start feeling you are wrong and that wrongness is natural: it is given to you, you are born with it, and you cannot immediately do anything about it. You cannot transform it; it is not so easy. You can suppress it; that's easy.

So two things you can do: you can create a false face; you can pretend something you are not. That saves you. In the society you can move more easily, more conveniently. And inwardly you have to suppress the real, because the unreal can be imposed only if the real is suppressed. So your reality goes on moving downwards into the unconscious and your unreality becomes your conscious. Your unreal part becomes more prominent and the real recedes back. You are divided, and the more you try to pretend, the greater will be the gap.

The child is born one, whole. That's why every child is so beautiful. The beauty is because of wholeness. The child has no gap, no split, no divisions, no fragments. The child is one. The real and unreal are not there. The child is simply real, authentic. You cannot say the child is moral; the child is neither moral nor immoral. He is just unaware that there is anything moral or immoral. The moment he becomes aware, the split starts. Then the child starts behaving in unreal ways, because to be real becomes more and more difficult.

Of necessity this happens, remember, because the family has to regulate, the parents have to regulate. The child has to be civilized, educated, given manners, cultivated; otherwise it will be impossible for the child to move in the society. He has to be told, "Do this. Don't do that." And when we say, "Do this," the child's reality may not be ready to do it. It may not be real. There may not be any real desire within the child to do it. And when we say, "Don't do this or don't do that," the child's nature may like to do it.

We condemn the real and we enforce the unreal, because the unreal is going to be helpful in an unreal society, and the unreal is going to be convenient where everyone is false. The real is not going to be convenient. A *real* child will be in basic difficulty with the society, because the whole society is unreal. This is a vicious circle.

We are born in a society, and hitherto not a single society has existed on the earth which is real. This is vicious! A child is born in a society, and a society is already there with its fixed rules, regulations, behavior, moralities. . .the child has to learn.

When he grows he will become false. Then children will be born to him, and he will help make them false, and this goes on and on. What to do? We cannot change the society. Or, if we try to change the society, we will not be there when the society will be changed. It will take eternal time. What to do?

The individual can become aware of this basic split within: that the real has been suppressed and the unreal has been imposed. This is pain, this is suffering, this is hell. You cannot get any satisfaction through the unreal, because through the unreal only unreal satisfactions are possible. And this is natural. Only through the real can real satisfactions happen. Through the real you can reach reality; through the real you can reach the truth. Through the unreal you can reach more and more hallucinations, illusions, dreams. And through dreams, you can deceive yourself, but you can never be satisfied.

For example, in a dream if you feel thirsty you may dream you are drinking water. This will be helpful and convenient for the sleep to continue. If this dream is not there, where you dream that you are drinking water, your sleep will broken. A real thirst is there. It will break the sleep; the sleep will be disturbed. Dream is a help; it gives you the feeling that you are drinking water. But the water is false. Your thirst is simply deceived; it is not removed. You may continue to sleep, but the thirst is there, suppressed.

This is happening—not only in sleep: in our whole life this is happening. You are searching for things through the unreal personality, which is not there, just a facade. If you don't get them, you will be in misery; if you get them, then too you will be in misery. If you don't get them, the misery will be lesser, remember. If you get them, the misery will be deeper and more.

Psychologists say that because of this unreal personality, we basically never want to reach the goal—never want to reach, basically, because if you reach the goal you will be totally frustrated. We live in hope; in hope we can continue. Hope is a dream! You never reach the goal, so you never come to realize that the goal is false.

A poor man struggling for riches is more happy in the struggle, because there is hope. And with the unreal personality, only hope is happiness. If the poor man gets the riches, he will become hopeless. Now frustration will be the natural consequence. Riches are there, but no satisfaction. He has achieved the goal, but nothing has happened; his hopes are shattered. That's why the moment a society gets affluent, it becomes disturbed.

If America is so much disturbed today, it is because hopes are achieved, goals are achieved, and you now cannot deceive yourself any more. So if in America the younger generation is revolting against all the goals of the older generation, it is because of this: because they all proved nonsense.

In India we cannot conceive this. We cannot conceive young people voluntarily going poor, hippie—*voluntarily* going poor! We cannot conceive. We still have hope. We are hoping in the future, someday the country will become rich and then there will be heaven. The heaven is always in the hope.

Because of this unreal personality, whatsoever you try, whatsoever you do, whatsoever you seek, becomes unreal. Tantra says truth can happen to you only if you are again grounded in the real. But to be grounded in the real you have to be very courageous with yourself, because the unreal is convenient and the unreal is so much cultivated, your mind is so much conditioned, that you will become afraid of the real.

Someone has asked that "You said yesterday to be in the love act totally"—to enjoy it, to feel the bliss of it, to remain in it, and when the body starts shaking, be the shaking. So someone has asked, "What are you teaching us—indulgence? This is perversion!" This is the unreal personality speaking to you.

The unreal personality is always against enjoying anything. It is always against *you*. You must not enjoy. It is always for sacrificing things—sacrificing you, sacrificing yourself for others. It looks beautiful because we have been brought up in it: "Sacrifice yourself for others—this is altruism! If you are trying to enjoy yourself, this is selfish." And the moment someone says this is selfish, this becomes a sin.

But I tell you, Tantra is a basically different approach. Tantra says unless you can enjoy yourself you cannot help anyone to enjoy. Unless you are really contented with yourself, you cannot serve others; you cannot help others towards their contentment. Unless you are overflowing with your own bliss, you are a danger to society, because a person who sacrifices always becomes a sadist. If your mother goes on talking to you and saying that "I have sacrificed myself for you," she will torture you. If the husband goes on saying to the wife that "I am sacrificing," he will be a sadistic torturer, he will torture. The sacrifice is just a trick to torture the other.

So those who are always sacrificing are very dangerous, potentially dangerous. Be aware of them, and don't sacrifice. The very word is ugly. Enjoy yourself, be bliss-filled, and when you are overflowing with your bliss, that bliss will reach to others also. But that is not a sacrifice. No one is obliged to you; no one needs to thank you. Rather you will feel grateful to others because they have been participating in your bliss. Words like 'sacrifice', 'duty', 'service', are ugly, they are violent.

Tantra says: Unless *you* are filled with light, how can you help others to be enlightened? Be selfish—only then can you be altruistic, otherwise the whole concept of altruism is nonsense. Be happy—only then can you help others to be happy. If you are sad, unhappy, bitter, you are going to be violent with others and you will create misery for others.

You may become a *mahatma*—that is not very difficult—but look at your *mahatmas*. They are trying in every way to torture everyone who comes to them. But their torturing is very deceptive. They torture you "for your own sake"; they torture you "for your own good." And because they are torturing themselves you cannot say that "You are preaching something to us which you are not practicing." They are practicing it already. They are torturing themselves; now they can torture you. And when a torture is for your own good, that is the most dangerous torture— you cannot escape it.

And what is wrong in enjoying yourself? What is wrong in being happy? If there is anything wrong it is always in your unhappiness, because an unhappy person creates ripples of unhappiness all around him. Be happy! And the sex act, love, can be one of the deepest ways through which bliss can be attained.

Tantra is not teaching sexuality. It is simply saying that sex can be a source of bliss. And once you know *that* bliss, you can go further, because now you are grounded in reality. One is not to remain in sex forever, but you can use sex as a jumping board. That's what Tantra means: you can use it as a jumping board. And once you have known the ecstasy of sex, you can understand what mystics have been talking about—a greater orgasm, a cosmic orgasm.

Meera is dancing. You cannot understand her; you cannot even understand her songs. They *are* sexual, the symbology is sexual. It is bound to be, because in human life the sex act is the only act in which you come to feel a non-duality, in which you come to feel a deep oneness, in which the past disappears and the future disappears and only the present moment remains—the only real moment.

So all those mystics who have really known oneness with the divine, oneness with existence itself, they have always used sexual terms and symbols for their experience to express it. There is no other symbology; there is no other symbology which comes nearer to it.

Sex is just the beginning, not the end. But if you miss the beginning, you will miss the end also. And you cannot escape the beginning to reach the end.

Tantra says take life naturally; don't be unreal. Sex is there—a deep possibility, a great potentiality. Use it! And what is wrong in being happy in it? Really, all moralities are against happiness. Someone is happy and you feel something has gone wrong. When someone is sad, everything is okay. We live in a neurotic society where everyone is sad. When you are sad, everyone is happy because everyone can sympathize with you. When you are happy, everyone is at a loss—what to do with you? When someone sympathizes with you, look at his face. The face gleams; a subtle shining comes to the face. He is happy sympathizing. If *you* are happy, then there is no possibility—your happiness will create sadness in others, your unhappiness creates happiness. This is neurosis! The very foundation seems to be mad.

Tantra says be real, be authentic to yourself. Your happiness is not bad, it is good. It is not sin. Only sadness is sin, only to be miserable is sin. To be happy is virtue because a happy person will not create unhappiness for others. Only a happy person is and can be a ground for others' happiness.

Secondly, when I say Tantra is neither moral nor immoral, I mean Tantra is basically a science.

It sees in you what you are. It doesn't mean that Tantra is not trying to transform you, but it transforms you through reality. The difference is just like magic and science—that is the same difference between morality and Tantra. Magic also tries to transform things just through words, without knowing the reality. A magician can say that "Now the rains will stop." Really, he cannot stop them. Or he will say, "Now the rains will come." He cannot start them. He can just go on using words.

Sometimes coincidences will be there, and then he will feel powerful. And if the thing is not going to happen according to his magic prophecy, he can always say, "What has gone wrong?" That possibility is always hidden in his prophecy. With magic everything starts with 'if'. He can say, "If everyone is good, virtuous, then the rains will come on that particular day." If the rains come it is okay; if the rains are not coming, then everyone is not virtuous. There is someone who is a sinner.

Even in *this* century, the twentieth century, a person like Mahatma Gandhi could say, when there was a famine in Bihar, "It is because of the sins of the people living in Bihar that the famine has come"—as if the whole world is not sinning, only Bihar. Magic starts with 'if', and that 'if' is great and big.

Science never starts with 'if' because science first tries to know what is real—what reality is, what the real is. Once the real is known, it can be transformed. Once you know what electricity is, it can be changed, transformed, used. A magician doesn't know what electricity is. Without knowing electricity he is going to transform, he is thinking to transform! Those prophecies are just false, illusions.

Morality is just like magic. It goes on talking about the perfect man, and without knowing what man is—the real man. The perfect man remains as a dream. It is used just to condemn the real man. Man never reaches it.

Tantra is science. Tantra says first know what the reality is, what the man is. And don't create values and don't create ideals right now; first know what *is*. Don't think of the 'ought', just think of the 'is'. And once the 'is' is known, then you can change it. Now you have a secret.

For example, Tantra says don't try to go against sex, because if you go against sex and try to create a state of *brahmacharya*, celibacy, purity, it is impossible—it is just magical. Without knowing what sex energy is, without knowing what sex is constituted of, without going deep into the reality of it, the secrets of it, you can create an ideal of *brahmacharya*, but what will you do? You will simply suppress. And a person who is suppressing sex is more sexual than a person who is indulging in it, because through indulgence the energy is relieved, through suppression it is there moving in your system continuously.

A person who suppresses sex starts seeing sex everywhere. Everything becomes sexual. Not that everything is sexual, but now he projects. Now he projects! His own hidden energy now is projected. He will look everywhere and he will see everywhere sex. And because he is condemning himself, he will start condemning everyone. You cannot find a moralist who is not violently condemning; of everyone he is condemning—everyone is wrong. It feels good; his ego is fulfilled. But why is everyone wrong? Because everywhere he sees the same thing he is suppressing. His own mind will become more and more sexual, and more and more he will be afraid. This *brahmacharya* is perversion, unnatural.

A different type of *brahmacharya* of a different quality happens to the follower of Tantra. But the very process is totally, diametrically opposite. Tantra first teaches how to move in sex, how to know it, how to feel it, and how to come to the deepest possibility hidden in it, to the climax— how to find out the essential beauty, the essential happiness and bliss that is hidden there.

Once you know that secret you can transcend it, because really in deep sexual orgasm, it is not sex which gives you bliss; it is something else. Sex is just a situation. Something else is giving you the euphoria, the ecstasy. That something else can be divided into three elements. But when I say and describe those elements, don't think that you can understand them. They must become part of your experience. As concepts they are useless.

Because of three basic elements in sex, you come to a blissful moment. Those three are, first: timelessness. You transcend time completely. There is no time. You forget time completely; time ceases for you. Not that *time* ceases: it ceases for you; you are not in it. There is no past, no future. *This* very moment, here and now, the whole existence is concentrated. *This* moment becomes the only real moment. If you can make this moment the only real moment without sex, there is no need of sex. Through meditation it happens.

Secondly: in sex, for the first time, you lose your ego, you become egoless. So all those who are very much egoistic, they are always against sex, because in sex they have to lose their ego. You are not, neither is the other. You and your beloved both are lost into something else. A new reality evolves, a new unit comes into existence in which the old two are lost—completely lost. The ego is afraid. You are no more there. If, without sex, you can come to a moment where you are not, then there is no need.

And thirdly: for the first time, in sex you are natural. The unreal is lost; the facade, the face, is lost; the society, the culture, the civilization is lost. You are a part of nature—as trees are, animals are, stars are. You are a part of nature! You are in a greater something—the cosmos, the Tao. You are floating in it. You cannot even swim in it: you are not. You are just floating, you are taken by the current.

These three things give you the ecstasy. Sex is just a situation in which it happens naturally. Once you know and once you can feel these elements, you can create these elements independent of sex. All meditation is essentially the experience of sex without sex. But you have to *go* through it. It must become a part of *your* experience—not concepts, not ideas, not thoughts.

Tantra is not for sex, Tantra is to transcend. But you can transcend only through experience—existential experience—not through ideology. Only through Tantra does *brahmacharya* happen. This looks paradoxical, but it is not. Only through knowledge does transcendence happen. Ignorance cannot help you for transcendence; it can help you only for hypocrisy.

Now I will take the questions. Someone has asked:

> *How often should one indulge in sex in order to help and not hinder the meditation process?*

The question arises because we go on *mis*understanding. Your sex act and the Tantric sex act are basically different. Your sex act is to relieve. It is just like sneezing—a good sneeze. The energy is thrown out; you are unburdened. It is destructive, it is not creative. It is good, therapeutic; it helps you to be relaxed, but nothing more.

The Tantric sex act is basically, diametrically opposite and different. It is not to relieve; it is not to throw energy out. It is to remain in the act without ejaculation—without throwing energy out—remaining in the act merged, just the beginning part of the act, not the end part. It changes the quality; the complete quality is different then.

Try to understand two things. There are two types of climax, two types of orgasm. One type of orgasm is known: you reach to a peak of excitement, then you cannot go further; the end has come. The excitement reaches to a point where it becomes non-voluntary. The energy jumps in you and goes out. You are relieved of it, unburdened. The load is thrown; you can relax and sleep.

You are using it like a tranquilizer. It is a natural tranquilizer. A good sleep will follow—if your mind is not burdened by religion, then. Otherwise even the tranquilizer is destroyed. If your mind is not burdened by religion, only then can sex be a tranquilizing thing. If you feel guilt, your sleep will be disturbed. You will feel depression, you will start condemning yourself, and you will start taking oaths that now, no more. . . Your sleep will become a nightmare after it. If you are a natural being, not too much burdened by religion and morality, only then can sex be used as a tranquilizer.

This is one type of orgasm—coming to the peak of excitement. Tantra is centered on another type of orgasm. If we call the one 'peak', you can call it valley: not coming to the peak of excitement, but coming to the very deepest valley of relaxation. Excitement has to be used for both in the beginning; that's why I say in the beginning both are the same, but at the end they are totally different.

Excitement has to be used for both; either you are going towards the peak of excitement or to the valley of relaxation. For the first, excitement has to be intense—more and more intense. You have to grow in it; you have to help it to grow towards the peak. In the second, excitement is just the beginning. And once the man has entered, both lover and beloved can relax. No movement is needed. They can relax in a loving embrace. When the man feels or the woman feels that the erection is going to be lost, only then a little movement and excitement. . .but again relax. You can prolong this deep embrace for hours. No ejaculation. And then both can fall into a deep sleep, together. This is a valley orgasm. Both are relaxed and they meet as two relaxed beings.

In ordinary sexual orgasm you meet as two excited beings—tense, full of excitement, trying to unburden yourselves. Ordinary sexual orgasm looks mad. Tantric orgasm is a deep, relaxing meditation. Then there is no question. . .how often should one indulge? As much as you like, because no energy is lost. Rather, energy is gained.

You may not be aware of it but this is a fact of biology, bio-energy, that man and woman are opposite forces—negative/positive, yin/yang, or whatsoever you call them. They are challenging to each other, and when they both meet in a deep relaxation they revitalize each other. They both vitalize each other, they both become younger, they both feel livelier, they both become radiant with new energy. And nothing is lost! Just by meeting the opposite pole, energy is renewed.

The Tantra love act can be done as much as you like. The ordinary sex act cannot be done as much as you like, because you are losing energy and your body will have to wait to regain it. And only when you regain it can you lose it again. This looks absurd: the whole life spent regaining and losing, gaining and losing. It is just like an obsession.

Second thing to be remembered: you may have observed or may not have observed, if you look at animals; you will never see that they are enjoying; in intercourse they are not enjoying. Look at baboons, monkeys, dogs or any animal—in their sex act you cannot observe that they are feeling blissful or enjoying it. You cannot! It seems just a mechanical act, a natural force pushing them towards it. If you have seen monkeys in intercourse, after the intercourse they will separate. Look at their faces. There is no ecstasy—as if nothing has happened. When the energy forces, when the energy is too much, they throw it.

The ordinary sex act is just like this, and moralists have been saying quite the contrary. They say, "Don't indulge. Don't enjoy." They say, "This is like animals." This is not! Animals never enjoy—only man can enjoy. And the deeper you can enjoy, a higher humanity is born to you. And if your sex act can become meditative, ecstatic, the highest is touched.

But remember Tantra: it is a valley orgasm. It is not a peak experience, it is a valley experience.

In the West, Abraham Maslow has made this term 'peak experience' very famous. You go in excitement towards the peak, and then you fall. That's why, after every sex act, you feel a fall, and a depression. You are falling from a peak.

You will never feel that after a Tantra sex experience. You are not falling! You cannot fall any further—you have been in the valley. Rather, you are rising.

When you come back after a Tantra sex act, you have risen, not fallen. You feel filled with energy, more vital, more alive, radiant. And that ecstasy will last for hours, even for days. It depends how deep you were in it.

And if you can go, move in it, sooner or later you will realize ejaculation is wastage of energy. No need—unless you need children. And you will feel a deep relaxation the whole day. One Tantra sex experience, and for days you will feel relaxed, at ease, at home, non-violent, non-angry, non-depressed. And this type of person is never a danger to others. If he can, he will help others to be happy. If he cannot, at least he will not make anyone unhappy.

Only Tantra can create a new man. And a man who has known timelessness, egolessness and a deep non-duality with existence will grow now. A dimension has opened. It is not far away, the day is not very far away, when sex will simply disappear. When sex disappears without your knowledge, suddenly one day you realize that sex has disappeared completely and there is no lust, *brahmacharya* is born. But this is arduous—looks arduous because of too much false teaching. And you feel afraid also because of your mind conditioning.

Of two things we are very much afraid—sex and death. But both are basic, and a *really* religious seeker will enter both. He will experience sex to know what it is, because to know sex is to know life. And he will also like to know what death is, because unless death is known you cannot know what eternal life is. If I can enter sex to its very center, I know what life is. And if I can enter into death voluntarily, to its very center, the moment I touch the center of death I have become eternal. Now I am immortal because death is something that happens just on the periphery.

Sex and death both are basic for a real seeker, but for ordinary humanity both are taboo—don't talk about them. And both are basic and both are deeply related. They are so deeply related that even entering sex you enter a certain death, because you are dying. The ego is disappearing, time is disappearing, your individuality is disappearing—you are dying! Sex is also a subtle death. And if you can know that sex is a subtle death, death can become a great sexual orgasm.

A Socrates entering death is not afraid. Rather, he is very much enthusiastic, thrilled, excited, to know what death is. A deep welcome in his heart. Why? Because if you have known the small death of sex and you have known the bliss that follows it, you would like to know the greater death—a greater bliss is hidden behind it. But for us both are taboo. For Tantra, both are basic searching dimensions. One has to go through them.

Someone has asked:

> *If one experiences meditation as a rising of kundalini up the spinal passage, does it not deplete one's meditative energies to have orgasm?*

All the questions are basically without understanding what the Tantra sex act is. Ordinarily it is so. If your energy goes up, raises your kundalini and rushes up towards the head, you cannot have ordinary orgasm. And if you try to have, you will be in a deep conflict within, because energy is moving up and you are forcing it down. But the Tantra orgasm is not a difficulty; it will be a help.

Energy moving up is not contradictory to Tantra orgasm. You can relax, and that relaxation with your beloved will help the energy move higher. In the ordinary sex act it is a difficulty. That's why all those techniques which are not Tantric, they are against sex, because they don't know that a valley orgasm is possible. They know only one—ordinary orgasm—and then it is a problem for them. For Yoga it is a problem, because Yoga is trying to force your sex energy upwards. It is called kundalini—your sex energy moving upwards.

In the sex act it moves downwards. Yoga will say: Be a celibate, because if you are doing both you are creating chaos in your system. On the one hand trying to pull energy up and on the other hand throwing energy out, down, you are creating chaos. That's why Yoga techniques are against sex.

But Tantra is not against sex because Tantra has a different type of orgasm, a valley orgasm, which can help. And there is no chaos, no conflict created. Rather, it will be helpful. If you are escaping—if you are men and escaping women or if you are women escaping men—whatsoever you do the other remains in your mind and goes on pulling you down. This is paradoxical, but this is a truth.

While in deep embrace with your beloved you can forget the other. Only then do you forget the other. A man forgets that woman exists, a woman forgets that man exists. Only in deep embrace, the other is no more. And when the other is no more, your energy can flow easily; otherwise the other goes on pulling it down.

So Yoga and ordinary techniques escape from the other, the other sex. They have to escape, be aware, continuously struggling and controlling. But if you are against the other sex, that very 'againstness' is a constant strain and goes on pulling you down.

Tantra says no strain is needed. Be relaxed with the other. In that relaxed moment, the other disappears and your energy can flow up. But it flows up only when you are in a valley. It flows down when you are at a peak.

One question more:

> *Last night you said that the sexual act should be slow and unhurried, but you also said that one should not have any control over the sexual act and one should become total. It confuses me.*

It is not control. Control is a totally different thing and relaxation is different. You are *relaxing* in it, not controlling it. If you are controlling it, there will be no relaxation. If you are controlling it, sooner or later you will be hurried to finish it, because control is a strain. And every strain creates tension, and tension creates a necessity, a need, to release. It is not a control! You are not resisting something! You are simply not in a hurry, because sex is not to move somewhere. You are not going somewhere. It is just a play; there is no goal. Nothing is to be reached, so why hurry?

But man is always, in his every act, present totally. If you are hurried in everything, you will be hurried in your sex act also—because *you* will be there. A person who is very much time-conscious will be hurried in his sex act also, as if time is being wasted. So we ask for instant coffee and for instant sex. With coffee it is good, but with sex it is simply nonsense. There can be no instant sex. It is not work and it is not something which you can hurry. Through hurry you will destroy it; you will miss the very point. Enjoy it, because through it a timelessness is to be felt. If you are in a hurry, then timelessness cannot be felt.

When Tantra says go unhurriedly, slowly enjoying, just as if you are going for a walk in the morning, not going to the office, that is a different thing. When you are going to the office you are in a hurry to reach somewhere, and when you are on a walk in the morning you are not in a hurry because you are not going anywhere. You are simply going. There is no hurry, there is no goal. You can return from any point.

This unhurriedness is basic to create the valley; otherwise the peak will be created. And when this is said, it is not meant that you have to control. You are not to control your excitement, because that is contradictory. You cannot control excitement. If you control, you are creating a double excitement. Just relax, take it as a play— don't make any end. The beginning is enough!

In the act, close your eyes, feel the other's body, feel the other's energy flowing towards you, and be merged in it, melt in it. It will come! The old habit may persist for a few days. . .it will go. But don't force it to go. Just go on relaxing, relaxing, relaxing. And if there is no ejaculation, don't feel that something has gone wrong, because the man feels that something has gone wrong. If there is no ejaculation, he feels something has gone wrong. Nothing has gone wrong! And don't feel that you have missed something. You have not missed.

In the beginning it will be felt like missing something because the excitement and the peak will not be there. And before the valley comes you will feel that you are missing something, but this is just an old habit. Within a period, within a month, three weeks, the valley will start appearing. And when the valley appears, you will forget your peaks. No peak is worthwhile then. But you have to wait. And don't force it, and don't control. Just relax.

Relaxation is a problem—because when we say relax, in the mind it is translated as if some effort is to be made. Our language gives this appearance. I was reading one book; the book is entitled, "You Must Relax!" The 'must', the very 'must' will not allow you to relax, because then it becomes a goal—"You must!"—and if you are not able, you will feel frustrated. The very 'must' gives you a feeling of hard effort, an arduous journey. You cannot relax if you are thinking in terms of 'must'.

Language is a problem. For certain things, language always expresses wrongly. For example, relaxation: if I say to relax, then too it becomes an effort and you will ask, "How to relax?" With 'how' you miss the point. You cannot ask 'how'. You are asking for a technique: technique will create effort, effort will create tension. So if you ask me how to relax, I will say: Don't do anything. Just relax! Just lie down and wait. Don't do anything! All that you can do will be the barrier; it will create the hindrance.

If you start counting from one to a hundred and back from a hundred to one, you will remain awake the whole night. And if sometimes you have fallen asleep because of counting, it is not because of counting—it is because you counted and counted, and then you got bored, because you got bored. It is not because of counting, only because of boredom. Then you forgot counting and the sleep came. But sleep comes only, relaxation comes only when you are not doing anything. This is the problem.

When I say 'sex act', it looks like an effort. It is not! Just start playing with your beloved or your lover. Just go on playing, feel each other, be sensitive to each other, just like small children playing or just like dogs playing, animals playing. Just go on playing, and don't think about the sex act at all. It may happen, it may not happen.

If it happens through just playing, it will lead

you to the valley more easily. If you think about it, then you are already ahead of yourself: you are playing with your beloved but you are thinking of the sex act. Then the playing is false. You are not here, and the mind is in the future. And this mind will move always in the future.

When you are in the sex act, the mind is thinking how to finish it. It is always ahead of you. Don't allow it! Just play, and forget about any sex act. It will happen. Allow it to happen. Then it will be easy to relax. And when it happens. . .just relax. Be together. Be in each other's presence, and feel happy.

Negatively, something can be done. For example, when you get excited you breathe fast because excitement needs fast breathing. For relaxation, it is good, helpful, if you breathe deep —not fast, slow, breathing so easily, at ease. Then the sex act can be prolonged.

Don't talk, don't say anything, because that creates disturbance. Don't use mind, use bodies. Use mind only to feel what is happening. Don't think, just feel what is happening. The warmth that is flowing, the love that is flowing, the energy that is in contact, just feel it! Be aware of it. And that too should not be made a strain—effortlessly floating. Then only will the valley appear. And once the valley appears, you are transcending.

Once you feel and realize the valley, the relaxed orgasm, it is already a transcendence. The sex is not there. Now it has become a meditation, a samadhi.

Tantra - the Path of Surrender

"If love cannot help you into meditation nothing will help!"

The first question:

> *Bhagwan, please explain whether the techniques we have discussed until now in "Vigyan Bhairava Tantra" belong to the science of Yoga instead of the actual and central subject matter of Tantra. And what is the central subject matter of Tantra?*

THIS QUESTION arises to many. The techniques that we have discussed are also used by Yoga—the same techniques, but with a difference. You can use the same technique with a very different philosophy behind it. The framework, the background differs, not the technique. Yoga has a different attitude towards life, just the contrary to Tantra.

Yoga believes in struggle; Yoga is basically the path of will. Tantra doesn't believe in struggle; Tantra is not the path of will. Rather, on the contrary, Tantra is the path of total surrender. Your will is not needed. For Tantra your will is the problem, the source of all anguish. For Yoga, your surrender, your 'will-lessness', is the problem.

Because your will is weak, that's why you are in anguish, suffering—for Yoga. For Tantra, because you have the will, you have the ego, the individuality, that's why you are suffering. Yoga says bring your will to absolute perfection and you will be liberated. And Tantra says dissolve your will completely, become totally empty of it, and that will be your liberation. And both are right. . . This creates difficulty. For me, both are right.

But the path of Yoga is a very difficult one. It is just impossible, nearly impossible, that you can attain to the perfection of the ego. That means you have to become the center of the whole universe. The path is very long, arduous. And, really, never reaches to the end. So what happens to the followers of Yoga? Somewhere on the path, in some life, they turn to Tantra. That happens.

Intellectually it is conceivable; existentially it is

impossible. If it is possible, you will reach by Yoga also. But generally it never happens. Or even if it happens, it happens very rarely. A Mahavira. . .sometimes centuries and centuries pass and then a man like Mahavira attains through Yoga. But he is rare, the exception, and he proves the rule.

But Yoga is more attractive than Tantra. Tantra is easy, natural, and you can attain through Tantra very easily, very naturally, effortlessly. And because of this, Tantra never appeals to you so much. Why? Anything that appeals to you appeals to your ego. Whatsoever you feel is going to fulfill your ego will appeal to you more. You are gripped in the ego. Yoga appeals very much.

Really, the more egoistic you are, the more Yoga will appeal to you, because it is pure ego effort. The more impossible, the more appealing to the ego. That's why Everest has so much appeal; to reach to the top of the Himalayan peak, it is so difficult. And when Hillary and Tensing reached Everest, they felt a very ecstatic moment. What was that?—ego fulfilled. They were the first.

When the first man landed on the moon, can you imagine how *he* felt? He was the first in all

111

history. And now he cannot be replaced; he will remain the first in all the history to come. Now there is no way to change his status. The ego is fulfilled deeply. There is no competitor now and there cannot be. Many will land on the moon, but they will not be the first.

But many can land on the moon and many will go to Everest. Yoga gives you a higher peak and a more unreachable end: the perfection of the ego— pure, perfect, absolute ego.

Yoga would have appealed to Nietzsche very much because he said the energy that is working behind life is the energy of will—will to power. Yoga gives you the feeling that you are more powerful through it. The more you can control yourself, the more you can control your instincts, the more you can control your body, the more you can control your mind. . .you feel powerful. You become a master inside. But this is through conflict; this is through struggle and violence.

And it always happens more or less that a person who has been practicing for many lives through Yoga comes to a point where the whole journey becomes drab, dreary, futile, because the more ego is fulfilled, the more you will feel it is useless. And then the follower of the path of Yoga turns to Tantra.

112

But Yoga appeals because everyone is egoistic. Tantra never appeals in the beginning. Tantra can appeal only to the higher adepts—those who have worked on themselves, those who have been really struggling through Yoga for many lives. Then Tantra appeals to them because they can understand. Ordinarily, you will not be attracted by Tantra. Or, if you are attracted, you will be attracted by wrong reasons. So try to understand them also.

You will not be attracted by Tantra in the first place because it asks you to surrender, *not* to fight. It asks you to float, not to swim. It asks you to move with the current, not to go upstream. It tells you nature is good. Trust nature—don't fight it. Even sex is good. Trust it, follow it, flow into it —don't fight. *No*-fight is the central teaching of Tantra. Flow, let go!

It cannot appeal. There is no fulfillment of your ego through it. In the first step it asks for your ego to be dissolved. In the very beginning it asks you to dissolve it.

Yoga will also ask you, but at the end. First it will ask you to purify it. And when it is purified completely, it dissolves; it cannot remain. But that is the last in Yoga, and in Tantra that is the first.

113

So Tantra will not appeal generally. And if it does appeal, it will appeal for wrong reasons. For example, if you want to indulge in sex, then you can rationalize your indulgence through Tantra. That can become the appeal. If you want to indulge in wine and women and other things, you can feel attracted towards Tantra. But, really, you are not attracted towards Tantra—Tantra is a facade, a trick. You are attracted to something else which Tantra, *you* think, allows you. So Tantra always appeals for wrong reasons.

Tantra is not to help your indulgence, it is to transform it. So don't deceive yourself. Through Tantra you can deceive yourself very easily. And because of this possibility of deception, Mahavira would not prescribe Tantra. This possibility is always there. And man is so deceptive that he can show one thing for something else that he intends through it. He can rationalize.

For example in China, old China, there was something like Tantra, a secret science. It is known as Tao. Tao has similar trends to Tantra. For example, Tao says that it is good, if you want to be freed of sex, it is good that you should not stick to one person—one woman, one man. You should not stick to one if you want to be freed. So

Tao says it is better to go on changing partners.

This is absolutely right—but you can rationalize it, you can deceive yourself. You may just be a sex maniac and then you can think that "I am doing Tantra practice, so I cannot stick to one woman, I am to change." And many emperors in China practiced it. They had big harems only for this.

But Tao *is* meaningful—Tao is meaningful if you look deep down into human psychology. If you know only one woman, sooner or later your attraction for that woman will wither away, but your attraction for woman will remain. You will be attracted by the other sex, but this woman, your wife, really will not be of the opposite sex. She will not attract you, she will not be a magnet for you. You have become accustomed to her.

Tao says if a man moves amidst women, many women, he will not only be beyond one—he will go beyond the opposite sex. The very knowledge of many women will help him to transcend. And this is right, but dangerous, because you would like it not because it is right but because it gives you license. That is the problem with Tantra.

So in China also that knowledge was suppressed; it had to be suppressed. In India also,

Tantra was suppressed because it says many dangerous things—they are dangerous only because you are deceptive. Otherwise they are wonderful. Nothing has happened to the human mind more wonderful and mysterious than Tantra; no knowledge is so deep.

But knowledge always has its dangers. For example, now science has become a danger because it has given you very deep secrets. Now you know how to create atomic energy. Einstein is reported to have said that if he is given again a life, rather than being a scientist he would like to be a plumber, because as he looks back his whole life has been futile—not only futile, but dangerous to humanity. And he has given one of the deepest secrets, but to the man who is self-deceptive.

I wonder, the day may come soon when we will have to suppress scientific knowledge. There are rumors and there are secret thoughts amid scientists whether to disclose more or not—whether we should stop the search or should we go further?—because now it is dangerous ground.

Every knowledge is dangerous; only ignorance is not dangerous. You cannot do much with it. Superstitions are always good—never dangerous, homeopathic. Give the medicine. . .it is not going to harm you, one thing is certain. Whether it is going to help you or not depends on your own illusions. One thing is certain: it is not going to harm you. Homeopathy is harmless; it is a deep superstition. It can only help. Remember, if something can *only* help, then it is superstition. If it can do both, help and harm, then only is it knowledge.

A real thing can do both—help and harm. Only an unreal thing can just help. But then the help never comes from the thing. It is always a projection of your own mind. So unreal, illusory things are good in a way—they never harm you.

Tantra is science, and deeper than atomic knowledge—because atomic science is concerned with matter and Tantra is concerned with *you.* And you are always more dangerous than any atomic energy. Tantra is concerned with the biological atom, you—the living cell, life consciousness itself, and how it works, the inner mechanism.

That's why Tantra became so much interested in sex. One who is interested in life and consciousness will automatically become interested in sex, because sex is the source of life, of love, of all that is happening in the world of consciousness. So if a seeker is *not* interested in sex, he is not a seeker at all. He may be a philosopher, but

117

he is not a seeker. And philosophy is more or less nonsense—thinking about things which are of no use.

I have heard: Mulla Nasruddin was interested in a girl, but he had very bad luck with girls. No one would like him. And he was going to meet a girl for the first time, so he asked a friend, he said, "What is your secret? You are wonderful with women. You simply hypnotize them and I am always a failure—give me some clue. I am going on a date for the first time with this girl, so give me some secrets."

So the friend said, "Remember three things: always talk about food, family and philosophy."

"Why about food?" Mulla asked.

The friend said, "I talk about food because then the girl feels good—because every woman is interested in food. She is food for the child, for the whole humanity she is food, so she is basically interested in food."

Mulla said, "Okay. And why family?"

So the man said, "Talk about her family so your intentions look honorable."

Then Mulla asked, "And why about philosophy?"

The man said, "Talk about philosophy—that

118

makes the woman feel that she is intelligent."

So Mulla rushed. Immediately, the moment he saw the girl, he asked, "Hello, do you like noodles?"

The girl, startled, said, "No!"

So the Mulla asked the second question, "Have you got a brother?"

The girl was even more startled. . ."What type of date is this!" She said, "No!"

So for a moment Mulla was at a loss: "How to start on philosophy?" But he started—just for a moment he was at a loss and then he asked, "Now, if you had a brother would he like noodles?"

This is philosophy. Philosophy is more or less nonsense. Tantra is not interested in philosophy; Tantra is interested in actual, existential life. So Tantra never asks whether there is a God or whether there is *moksha* or whether there is a hell and heaven. No. Tantra asks basic questions about life. That's why so much interest in sex and love—they are *basic*. You *are* through them; you are part of them.

You are a play of sex energy and nothing else. And unless you understand *this* energy *and* transcend it, you will never be anything more. You are, right now, nothing but sex energy. You can be more, but if you don't understand this and don't transcend it, you will never be more. The possibility is just a seed.

That's why Tantra is interested in sex, in love, in natural life. But the way to know it is not conflict. Tantra says you cannot know anything if you are in a fighting mood—then you are not receptive. Then because you are fighting the secrets will be hidden from you. You are not open to receive them.

And when you are fighting you are always outside. If you are fighting sex, *you* are always outside. If you surrender to sex, you reach the very inner core of it, you are an insider. And if you surrender many things become known.

You have been in sex, but always with a fighting attitude behind. That's why you have not known many secrets. For example, you have not known the life-giving forces of sex—you have not known because you cannot know. That needs an insider.

If you are really floating with sex energy, totally surrendered, sooner or later you will arrive at the point when you know that sex cannot only give birth to a new life: sex can give you *more* life. To the lovers sex can become a life-giving force, but for that you need a surrender. And once surrendered, many dimensions change.

For example, Tantra has known, Tao has known, that if in the sex act you ejaculate then it cannot be life-giving to you. There is no need to ejaculate; ejaculation can be totally forgotten. Tantra and Tao both say ejaculation is because you are fighting; otherwise there is no need.

The lover and the beloved can be in a deep sexual embrace, just relaxing into each other with no hurry to ejaculate, with no hurry to end up the affair. They can just relax into each other. And if this relaxation is total, they both will feel more life. They both will enrich each other.

Tao says a man can live for one thousand years if he is not in any hurry with sex, just deeply relaxed. If a woman and a man are deeply relaxed with each other, simply meeting with each other, absorbed into each other, not in any hurry, not in any tension, many things happen, alchemical things happen—because the life juices of both meet, the electricity of both, the bio-energy of both, meet. And just by this meeting (because they are 'anti'—one is negative, one is positive: they are anti-poles), just by meeting with each other deeply, they invigorate each other, make each other vital, more alive.

They can live for long and they can live never becoming old. But this can only be known if you are not in a fighting mood. And this seems paradoxical. Those who are fighting sex, they will ejaculate sooner, because the tense mind is in a hurry to be relieved of the tension.

New research says many surprising things, many surprising facts. Masters and Johnson, they have worked scientifically for the first time with what happens in deep intercourse. They have come to realize that seventy-five percent of men are premature ejaculators—seventy-five percent of men! Before there is a deep meeting, they have ejaculated and the act is finished. And ninety percent of women never achieve any orgasm; they never reach to a peak, a deep, fulfilling peak —ninety percent of women!

That's why women are so angry, irritated, and they will remain so. No meditation can help them easily and no philosophy, no religion, no ethics, will make them at ease with the men they are living with. And then their frustration, their anger . . .because modern science and old Tantra both say that unless a woman is deeply fulfilled, orgasmic, she will be a problem in the family. That which she is lacking will create irritations and she will be always in a fighting mood.

So if your wife is always in a fighting mood, think again about the whole thing. It is not simply the wife—you may be the cause. And because women are not achieving orgasm, they become anti-sex. They are not willing to go into sex easily. They have to be bribed; they are not ready to go into sex. Why should they be ready, because they never achieve any deep bliss through it? Rather, they feel after it that the man has been using them, they have been used. They feel like a thing used and then discarded.

The man is satisfied because he has ejaculated. Then he moves and goes to sleep, and the wife goes on weeping. She has been just *used,* and the experience has not been in any way fulfilling to her. It may have relieved her husband or lover or friend, but it has not been in any way fulfilling to her.

Ninety percent of women don't even know what orgasm is, because they have never known it; they have never reached a peak of such a blissful convulsion of the body that every fiber vibrates and every cell becomes alive. They have not reached it, and this is because of an anti-sexual attitude in the society. The fighting mind is there, so the woman is so repressed she has become frigid.

123

And the man goes on doing the act as if it is a sin. He feels guilty; he knows "it is not to be done." And while he is making love to his wife or beloved, he is thinking of some *mahatma:* "How to go to the *mahatma* and how to transcend this sex, this guilt, this sin."

It is very difficult to get rid of the *mahatmas;* they are always there. Even while you are making love you are not two—one *mahatma* must be there, you are three. And if there is no *mahatma,* then God is watching you doing this sin. The concept of God in people's minds is just that of a Peeping Tom who is always watching you. This attitude creates anxiety. And when anxiety is there, ejaculation comes soon.

When there is no anxiety, ejaculation can be postponed for hours—even for days. And there is no need! If the love is deep and both bodies can invigorate each other, then ejaculation may completely cease. For years two lovers can meet with each other without any ejaculation, without any wastage of energy. They can just relax with each other. Their bodies meet and relax; they enter and relax. And sooner or later, sex then is not an excitement. It is an excitement right now. Then it is not an excitement, it is a relaxation, a deep let-go.

But that can happen only if first you have surrendered inside to the life energy—the life force. Only then can you surrender to your lover or beloved.

Tantra says if this happens. . .and this Tantra arranges, how it can happen. Tantra says never make love while you are excited. This seems very absurd because you want to make love when you are excited, and both partners excite each other so that they can make love. But Tantra says in excitement you are wasting energy. Make love while you are calm, serene, meditative. First meditate, then make love. And in love also, don't go beyond the limit. What do I mean?—"don't go beyond the limit." Don't become excited and violent, so your energy is not dispersed.

If you see two persons making love you will feel they are fighting. Small children, if sometimes they see their father and mother, they think the father is going to kill the mother. It looks violent; it looks like a fight. It is not beautiful; it looks ugly.

It must be more musical, harmonious. The two partners must be as if they are dancing, not fighting—singing one harmonious melody, just creating an atmosphere in which they both will dissolve and become one. And then they relax. This is what Tantra means. Tantra is not sexual at all. Tantra is the *least* sexual thing, and so much concerned with sex. And if through this relaxation, let-go, nature reveals to you its secrets, it is no wonder. Then you begin to be aware what is happening. And in that awareness of what is happening many secrets come to your mind.

First, sex becomes life-giving. As it is now, it is death-giving. You are simply dying through it, wasting yourself, deteriorating. Secondly, it becomes the deepest natural meditation. Your thoughts cease completely. When you are relaxed with a lover totally, your thoughts cease, the mind is not there. Only your heart beats—the mind is *not* there. It becomes a natural meditation. And if love cannot help you into meditation, nothing will help, because everything else is just superfluous, superficial. If love cannot help, nothing will help!

Love has its own meditation. But you don't know love, you know only sex—and you know the misery of wasting energy. Then you get depressed after it. Then you decide to take the vow of *brahmacharya*. And this vow is taken in depression, this vow is taken in anger, this vow is taken in frustration. This is not going to help.

A vow can be helpful if taken in a very deep, relaxed, meditative mood—then! Otherwise you are simply showing your anger, frustration, and nothing else, and you will forget the vow within twenty-four hours. The energy will have come again, and just as an old routine you will have to relieve it.

So sex for you is nothing but something like a sneeze. You feel excited, and then when you sneeze out you feel relaxed. Something that was bothering in the nose is relieved—so something bothering at the sex center is relieved.

Tantra says sex is very deep because it is life, but you can be interested for wrong reasons. Don't be interested in Tantra for wrong reasons, and then you will not feel that Tantra is dangerous—then Tantra is life transforming.

Those methods we have been talking about have been used by Yoga also, but with a conflict, with a fighting attitude. Tantra uses the *same* methods, but with a very loving attitude. And that makes a great difference. The very quality of the technique changes. The technique becomes different because the whole background is different.

And you have asked:

What is the central subject matter of Tantra?

You! You are the central subject matter of Tantra—what you are right now and what is hidden in you that can grow, what you are and what you can be. Right now you are a sex unit. And unless this unit is understood deeply, you cannot become a spirit; you cannot become a spiritual unit. Sexuality and spirituality are two ends of one energy.

Tantra starts with you as you are, Yoga starts with you as your possibility is. Yoga starts with the end, Tantra starts with the beginning. And it is good to start with the beginning. It is always good to begin with the beginning, because if the end is the beginning, then you are creating unnecessary misery for yourself. You are not that—just the ideal. You have to become a god, the ideal, and you are just an animal. And this animal goes berserk because of the ideal of the god. It goes mad, it becomes crazy.

Tantra says forget the god. If you are the animal, understand this animal in its totality. In that understanding itself, the god will grow. And if it cannot grow through that understanding, then forget it; it can never grow. Ideals cannot bring

128

your possibilities out; only the knowledge of the real will help. So *you* are the central subject matter of Tantra—as you are and as you can become, your actuality and your possibility. They are the subject matter.

Sometimes people get worried. If you go to understand Tantra, God is not discussed, *moksha* is not discussed, *nirvana* is not discussed. What type of religion is Tantra? Tantra discusses things which make you feel disgusted; you won't like to discuss them. Who wants to discuss sex? Because everyone thinks he knows. Because you can reproduce, do you think you know?

Nobody wants to discuss sex and sex is the problem of everybody. Nobody wants to discuss love because everyone feels he is a great lover already. And look at your life! It is just hatred and nothing else. And whatsoever you call love is nothing but a relaxation, a little relaxation, of the hatred. Look around you, and then you will know what you know and what you don't know.

I am reminded. . .I have heard about one Jewish, Hassid teacher, Baal Shem: He was going every day to his tailor for a robe, and the tailor took six months to make a simple robe for the fakir, for the poor fakir! When the robe was ready and the tailor gave it to Baal Shem, Baal Shem asked, "Tell me, even God had only six days to create the world. Within six days God created the whole world and you took six months to make this poor man's robe?"

Baal Shem remembered the tailor in his memoirs. The tailor said, "Yes, God created the world in six days, but look at the world—what type of world he has created! Yes, he created the world in six days, but look at the world!"

Look around you; look at the world you have created. Then you will come to know that you don't know anything. You are just groping in the dark. And because everyone else also is groping in the dark, it cannot mean that you are living in light. Because everyone else is also groping the dark you feel good, because there is no comparison.

But you are in the dark, and Tantra starts with you as you are. Tantra wants to enlighten you about basic things which you cannot deny. Or if you try to deny them, it is at your own cost.

Second question:

> *How can one convert the sexual act into a medi-*
> *tative experience? Should one practice special*
> *positions in sex?*

Positions are irrelevant; positions are not
very meaningful. The real thing is the attitude
of the mind—not the position of the body, but
the position of the mind. But if you change
your mind you may want to change your positions, because they are related. But they are not
basic.

For example, the man is always on the woman
—on top of the woman. This is an egoist posture
because the man always feels he is better, superior, higher. How can he be below the woman?
But all over the world, in primitive societies, the
woman is above the man. So in Africa this posture
is known as the missionary posture—because for
the first time when missionaries, Christian missionaries, went to Africa, the primitives just
couldn't understand: "What are they doing? They
will kill the woman!"

It is known in Africa as the missionary posture.
African primitives say this is violent—that the

man should be on top of the woman. She is weaker, delicate—she must be on top of the man. But it is difficult for man to think of himself lower than woman, under her.

If your mind changes, many things will change —*many* things will change. It is better that the woman should be on top, for many reasons. Because if the woman is on top. . .she is passive, she is not going to do much violence. She will simply relax. And the man under her cannot do much—he will have to relax. It is good. If he is on top he is going to be violent. He will do much, and nothing on your part is needed to be done. For Tantra you have to relax, so it is good that the woman should be on top. She can relax better than any man. The feminin psychology is more passive, so relaxation comes easy.

Positions will change, but don't be bothered about positions much. First change your mind. Surrender to the life force; float in it. Sometimes, if you are *really* surrendered, your bodies will take the right position that is needed in that moment. If both partners are deeply surrendered, then their bodies will take the *right* posture that is needed in that moment.

And every day situations change, so there is no

need to fix it beforehand. That is the fault—that you try to fix. Whenever you try to fix, it is fixing by the mind. Then you are not surrendering.

If you surrender, then let things take their own shape. And there is a wonderful harmony—when both partners have surrendered, they will take many postures or they will not take them and just relax. But that depends on the life force, not on your cerebral decision beforehand. You need not decide anything beforehand! That decision is the problem. Even to make love, you decide. Even to make love, you go and consult books. There are books on how to make love. This shows what type of human mind we have produced—how to make love. Then it becomes cerebral; you think everything. Really, you do a rehearsal in the mind and then you enact it. It is a copy; it is never real then. You are enacting a rehearsal. It becomes acting; it is not authentic.

Just surrender and move with the force wherever it leads. What is the fear? Why be afraid? If with your lover you cannot be unafraid, then where will you be unafraid? And once you have the feeling that the life force helps itself and takes the *right* path that is needed, that will give you a very basic insight into the whole life. Then you can leave your whole life to the divine. That is your beloved.

Then you leave your whole life to the divine. Then you don't think and you don't plan. You don't force the future according to you. You just allow yourself to move into the future according to him, according to the total.

But how to make the sexual act meditation? Just by surrendering it becomes. Don't think about it—let it happen. And you be relaxed; don't move ahead. This is one of the basic problems with the mind: it always moves ahead. It is always seeking the result, and the result is in the future. So you are never in the act; you are always in the future seeking a result. That seeking a result will disturb everything; it damages everything.

Just be in the act. Forget the future! It is to come: you need not worry about it. And with your worries you are not going to bring it. It is already coming; it has already come. You forget about it. You just be here and now.

And sex can become a deep insight into being here and now. That is, I think, the only act now left in which you can be here and now. You cannot be here and now while in your office; you cannot be here and now while you are studying in your college; you cannot be here and now anywhere in this modern world. Only in love can you be here and now.

But even there you are not. You are thinking of the result. And now many modern books have created many new problems. Because you read a book on how to make love, then you are afraid whether you are making it right or wrong. You read a book on how a posture is to be taken, what type of posture, and then you are afraid whether you are taking the right posture or not.

Psychologists have created new worries in the mind. Now they say the husband must remember whether his wife is achieving orgasm or not, so he is worried: "Is my wife achieving orgasm or not?" And *this* worry is not going to help anyway; it will become the hindrance.

And now the wife is worried whether she is helping the husband to relax totally or not. So she must smile, or she must show that she is feeling very blissful. Everything becomes false! Both are worried about the result. And because of this worry those results will never come.

Forget everything. Flow in the moment and allow your bodies—your bodies know well; they have their own wisdom. Your bodies are constituted of sex cells. They have a built-in program; you are not asked at all. Just leave it to the body, and the body will move. This leaving altogether, this let-go, will create the meditation automatically.

And if you can feel it in sex, then you know one thing: that whenever you can surrender you will feel the same. Then you can surrender to a Master —it is a love relationship. You can surrender to a Master, and then, while you are putting your head at his feet, your head will become empty. You will be in meditation.

Then there is no need even of a Master—you can just go out and surrender to the sky. *You know how to surrender*, that's all. You can go and you can surrender to a tree. . . And that's why it looks foolish, because we don't know how to surrender. We see a person—a primitive man, a villager—going to the river, surrendering himself to the river, calling the river 'the Mother', 'the divine Mother', or surrendering to the rising sun, and calling the rising sun a great god, or going to a tree and putting his head on the roots and surrendering.

For us it becomes superstitious. You say,

"What nonsense are you doing? What will the tree do? What will the river do? They are not goddesses. And what is the sun? The sun is not a god." Anything becomes a god if you can surrender. So your surrender creates divinity. There is nothing divine; there is only a surrendering mind which creates divinity.

Surrender to your wife and she becomes divine; surrender to your husband, he becomes divine. The divinity is revealed through surrender. Surrender to a stone and there is no stone now—the stone has become a statue, alive, a person.

So just to know how to surrender. . . And when I say "how to surrender," I don't mean to know the technique. I mean you have got a natural possibility of surrendering in love. Surrender there and feel it there. And then, let it be spread all over your life.

BOOKS PUBLISHED BY
RAJNEESH FOUNDATION
INTERNATIONAL

For a complete catalog of all the books published by **Rajneesh** Foundation International, contact:

Rajneesh Foundation International
P.O. Box 9
Rajneeshpuram, Oregon 97741 USA
(503) 489-3462 (or 3411)

EARLY DISCOURSES

A Cup of Tea
letters to disciples

From Sex to Superconsciousness

THE BAULS

The Beloved (2 volumes)

BUDDHA

The Book of the Books (volume 1)
the Dhammapada

The Diamond Sutra
the Vajrachchedika Prajnaparamita Sutra

The Discipline of Transcendence (4 volumes)
the Sutra of 42 Chapters

The Heart Sutra
the Prajnaparamita Hridayam Sutra

BUDDHIST MASTERS

The Book of Wisdom (volume 1)
Atisha's Seven Points of Mind Training

The White Lotus
the sayings of Bodhidharma

HASIDISM

The Art of Dying

The True Sage

JESUS

Come Follow Me (4 volumes)
the sayings of Jesus

I Say Unto You (2 volumes)
the sayings of Jesus

KABIR

The Divine Melody

Ecstasy: The Forgotten Language

The Fish in the Sea is Not Thirsty

The Guest

The Path of Love

The Revolution

RESPONSES TO QUESTIONS

Be Still and Know

The Goose is Out

My Way: The Way of the White Clouds

Walking in Zen, Sitting in Zen

Walk Without Feet, Fly Without Wings
and Think Without Mind

Zen: Zest, Zip, Zap and Zing

SUFISM

Just Like That

The Perfect Master (2 volumes)

The Secret

Sufis: The People of the Path (2 volumes)

Unio Mystica (2 volumes)
the Hadiqa of Hakim Sanai

Until You Die

The Wisdom of the Sands (2 volumes)

TANTRA

The Book of the Secrets (volumes 4 & 5)
Vigyana Bhairava Tantra

Tantra, Spirituality & Sex
Excerpts from The Book of the Secrets

The Tantra Vision (2 volumes)
the Royal Song of Saraha

TAO

The Empty Boat
the stories of Chuang Tzu

The Secret of Secrets (2 volumes)
the Secret of the Golden Flower

Tao: The Pathless Path (2 volumes)
the stories of Lieh Tzu

Tao: The Three Treasures (4 volumes)
the Tao Te Ching of Lao Tzu

When The Shoe Fits
the stories of Chuang Tzu

THE UPANISHADS

The Ultimate Alchemy (2 volumes)
Atma Pooja Upanishad

Vedanta: Seven Steps to Samadhi
Akshya Upanishad

WESTERN MYSTICS

The Hidden Harmony
the fragments of Heraclitus

The New Alchemy: To Turn You On
Mabel Collins' Light on the Path

Philosophia Perennis (2 volumes)
the Golden Verses of Pythagoras

Guida Spirituale
the Desiderata

Theologia Mystica
the treatise of St. Dionysius

YOGA

Yoga: The Alpha and the Omega
(10 volumes)
the Yoga Sutras of Patanjali

ZEN

Ah, This!

Ancient Music in the Pines

And the Flowers Showered

Dang Dang Doko Dang

The First Principle

The Grass Grows By Itself

Nirvana: the Last Nightmare

No Water No Moon

Returning to the Source

A Sudden Clash of Thunder

The Sun Rises in the Evening

Zen: The Path of Paradox (3 volumes)

ZEN MASTERS

Hsin Hsin Ming: The Book of Nothing
(Original title: Neither This nor That)
The faith mind of Sosan

The Search
the Ten Bulls of Zen

Take It Easy (2 volumes)
poems of Ikkyu

This Very Body the Buddha
Hakuin's Song of Meditation

Zorba the Buddha
(January 1979)

The Sound of One Hand Clapping
(March 1981)

OTHER TITLES

Rajneeshism
*an introduction to Bhagwan
Shree Rajneesh and His Religion*

The Sound of Running Water
*a photobiography of Bhagwan
Shree Rajneesh and His work*

The Orange Book
*the meditation techniques of Bhagwan
Shree Rajneesh*

BOOKS FROM OTHER PUBLISHERS

ENGLISH EDITIONS
UNITED KINGDOM

The Art of Dying
(Sheldon Press)

The Book of the Secrets (volume 1)
(Thames & Hudson)

Dimensions Beyond the Known
(Sheldon Press)

The Hidden Harmony
(Sheldon Press)

Meditation: The Art of Ecstasy
(Sheldon Press)

The Mustard Seed
(Sheldon Press)

Neither This Nor That
(Sheldon Press)

No Water No Moon
(Sheldon Press)

Roots and Wings
(Routledge & Kegan Paul)

Straight to Freedom (Original title:
Until You Die)
(Sheldon Press

The Supreme Doctrine
(Routledge & Kegan Paul)

The Supreme Understanding (Original title:
Tantra: The Supreme Understanding)
(Sheldon Press)

Tao: The Three Treasures (volume 1)
(Wildwood House)

UNITED STATES OF AMERICA

The Book of the Secrets (volumes 1-3)
(Harper & Row)

The Great Challenge
(Grove Press)

Hammer on the Rock
(Grove Press)

I Am The Gate
(Harper & Row)

Journey Toward the Heart (Original title:
Until You Die)
(Harper & Row)

Meditation: The Art of Ecstasy
(Harper & Row)

The Mustard Seed
(Harper & Row)

My Way: The Way of the White Clouds
(Grove Press)

Only One Sky (Original title:
Tantra: The Supreme Understanding)
(Dutton)

The Psychology of the Esoteric
(Harper & Row)

Roots and Wings
(Routledge & Kegan Paul)

The Supreme Doctrine
(Routledge & Kegan Paul)

Words Like Fire (Original title:
Come Follow Me, volume 1)
(Harper & Row)

Bhagwan Shree Rajneesh, Een Introductie
by Swami Deva Amrito (Jan Foudraine)
(Ankh-Hermes)

Oorspronkelijk Gezicht, Een Gang naar Huis
by Swami Deva Amrito (Jan Foudraine)
(Ambo)

FRENCH

TRANSLATIONS

L'éveil à la Conscience Cosmique
(Dangles)

Je Suis La Porte
(EPI)

Le Livre des Secrets (volume 1)
(Soleil Orange)

La Meditation Dynamique
(Dangles)

The Orange Book
(Soleil Orange)

GERMAN

TRANSLATIONS

Auf der Suche
(Sambuddha Verlag)

Das Buch der Geheimnisse (volume 1)
(Heyne Verlag)

Das Orangene Buch
(Sambuddha Verlag)

Der Freund
(Sannyas Verlag)

Dimension Jenseits
(Sannyas Verlag)

Ekstase: Die vergessene Sprache
(Herzschlag Verlag, formerly Ki-Buch)

Esoterische Pyschologie
(Sannyas Verlag)

Die Rebellion der Seele
(Sannyas Verlag)

Ich bin der Weg
(Sannyas Verlag)

Intelligenz des Herzens
(Herzschlag Verlag, formerly Ki-Buch)

Jesus aber Schwieg
(Sannyas Verlag)

Kein Wasser Kein Mond
(Herzschlag Verlag, formerly Ki-Buch)

Komm und folge mir
(Sannyas Verlag)

Meditation: Die Kunst zu sich
selbst zu finden
(Heyne Verlag)

Mein Weg: Der Weg der weissen Wolke
(Herzschlag Verlag, formerly Ki-Buch)

Mit Wurzeln und mit Flügeln
(Edition Lotus)

Nicht bevor du stirbst
(Edition Gyandip, Switzerland)

Die Schuhe auf dem Kopf
(Edition Lotus)

Das Klatschen der einen Hand
(Edition Gyandip, Switzerland)

Spirituelle Entwicklung
(Fischer)

Sprengt den Fels der Unbewusstheit
(Fischer)

Tantra: Die höchste Einsicht
(Sambuddha Verlag)

Tantrische Liebeskunst
(Sannyas Verlag)

Die Alchemie der Verwandlung
(Edition Lotus)

Die verborgene Harmonie
(Sannyas Verlag)

Was ist Meditation?
(Sannyas Verlag)

BOOKS ON BHAGWAN

Begegnung mit Niemand
by Mascha Rabben (Ma Hari Chetana)
(Herzschlag Verlag)

Ganz entspannt im Hier und Jetzt
by Swami Satyananda
(Rowohlt)

Im Grunde ist alles ganz einfach
by Swami Satyananda
(Ullstein)

Wagnis Orange
by Ma Satya Bharti
(Fachbuchhandlung für Psychologie)

Wenn das Herz frei wird
by Ma Prem Gayan (Silvie Winter)
(Herbig)

GREEK

TRANSLATION

I Krifi Armonia (The Hidden Harmony)
(Emmanual Rassoulis)

HEBREW

TRANSLATION

Tantra: The Supreme Understanding
(Massada)

ITALIAN

TRANSLATIONS

L'Armonia Nascosta (volumes 1 & 2)
(Re Nudo)

Dieci Storie Zen di Bhagwan Shree Rajneesh
(Né Acqua, Né Luna)
(Il Fiore d'Oro)

La Dottrina Suprema
(Rizzoli)

Dimensioni Oltre il Conosciuto
(Mediterranee)

Io Sono La Soglia
(Mediterranee)

Il Libro Arancione
(Mediterranee)

Il Libro dei Segreti
(Bompiani)

Meditazione Dinamica:
    L'Arte dell'Estasi Interiore
(Mediterranee)

La Nuova Alchimia
(Psiche)

La Rivoluzione Interiore
(Mediterranee)

La Ricerca
(La Salamandra)

Il Seme della Ribellione (volumes 1-3)
(Re Nudo)

Tantra: La Comprensione Suprema
(Bompiani)

Tao: I Tre Tesori (volumes 1-3)
(Re Nudo)

Tecniche di Liberazione
(La Salamandra)

Semi di Saggezza
(SugarCo)

BOOKS ON BHAGWAN

Alla Ricerca del Dio Perduto
by Swami Deva Majid
(SugarCo)

Il Grande Esperimento: Meditazioni
    e Terapie nell'Ashram
    Di Bhagwan Shree Rajneesh
by Ma Satya Bharti
(Armenia)

L'Incanto D'Arancio
by Swami Swatantra Sarjano
(Savelli)

JAPANESE

TRANSLATIONS

Dance Your Way to God
(Rajneesh Publications)

The Empty Boat (volumes 1 & 2)
(Rajneesh Publications)

From Sex to Superconsciousness
(Rajneesh Publications)

The Grass Grows by Itself
(Fumikura)

The Heart Sutra
(Merkmal)

Meditation: The Art of Ecstasy
(Merkmal)

The Mustard Seed
(Merkmal)

My Way: The Way of the White Clouds
(Rajneesh Publications)

The Orange Book
(Wholistic Therapy Institute)

The Search
(Merkmal)

The Secret
(Merkmal)

Take It Easy (volume 1)
(Merkmal)

Tantra: The Supreme Understanding
(Merkmal)

Tao: The Three Treasures (volumes 1-4)
(Merkmal)

Until You Due
(Fumikura)

PORTUGUESE (BRAZIL)

TRANSLATIONS

O Cipreste No Jardim
(Soma)

Dimensões Além do Conhecido
(Soma)

O Livro Dos Segredos (volume 1)
(Maha Lakshmi Editora)

Eu Sou A Porta
(Pensamento)

A Harmonia Oculta
(Pensamento)

Meditacão: A Arte Do Extase
(Cultrix)

Meu Caminho: O Comainho
   Das Nuvens Brancas
(Tao Livraria & Editora)

Nem Agua, Nem Lua
(Pensamento)

O Livro Orange
(Soma)

Palavras De Fogo
(Global/Ground)

A Psicologia Do Esotérico
(Tao Livraria & Editora)

A Semente De Mostarda (volumes 1 & 2)
(Tao Livraria & Editora)

Tantra: Sexo E Espiritualidade
(Agora)

Tantra: A Suprema Compreensão
(Cultrix)

Antes Que Você Morra
(Maha Lakshmi Editora)

SPANISH

TRANSLATIONS

Introducción al Mundo del Tantra
(Collección Tantra)

Meditación: El Arte del Extasis
(Collección Tantra)

Psicología de lo Esotérico:
La Nueva Evolución del Hombre
(Cuatro Vientos Editorial)

¿Qué Es Meditación?
(Koan/Roselló Impresions)

Yo Soy La Puerta
(Editorial Diana)

Sólo Un Cielo (volumes 1 & 2)
(Colección Tantra)

BOOKS ON BHAGWAN

Il Riesgo Supremo
by Ma Satya Bharti
(Martinez Roca)

SWEDISH

TRANSLATION

Den Väldiga Utmaningen
(Livskraft)

RAJNEESH MEDITATION CENTERS, ASHRAMS AND COMMUNES

There are hundreds of Rajneesh meditation centers throughout the world. These are some of the main ones, which can be contacted for the name and address of the center nearest you. They can also tell you about the availability of the books of Bhagwan Shree Rajneesh — in English or in foreign language editions. General information is available from Rajneesh Foundation International.

Meditation and inner growth programs are available at: RAJNEESH INSTITUTE FOR THERAPY and RAJNEESH INSTITUTE FOR MEDITATION AND INNER GROWTH at Rajneeshpuram. For further information, contact:

RAJNEESH INSTITUTE FOR THERAPY
P.O. Box 9, Rajneeshpuram, Oregon 97741
USA
Tel: (503) 489-3328 (or 3411)

USA

RAJNEESH FOUNDATION INTERNATIONAL
P.O. Box 9, Rajneeshpuram, Oregon 97741
Tel: (503) 489-3301

DEEPTA RAJNEESH MEDITATION CENTER
3024 Ashby Avenue, Berkeley, CA 94705
Tel: (415) 845-2515

SAMBODHI RAJNEESH SANNYAS ASHRAM
Conomo Point Road, Essex, MA 01929 Tel: (617) 768-7640

UTSAVA RAJNEESH MEDITATION CENTER
20062 Laguna Canyon, Laguna Beach, CA 92651
Tel: (714) 497-4877

ABHINAVA RAJNEESH MEDITATION CENTER
701 Mission Street, Santa Cruz, CA 95060
Tel: (408) 427-0188

DEVADEEP RAJNEESH SANNYAS ASHRAM
1403 Longfellow St., N.W., Washington, D.C. 20011
Tel: (202) 723-2186

CANADA

ARVIND RAJNEESH SANNYAS ASHRAM
2807 W. 16th Ave., Vancouver, B.C. V6K 3C5
Tel: (604) 734-4681

SHANTI SADAN RAJNEESH MEDITATION CENTER
1817 Rosemont, Montreal, Quebec H2G 1S5
Tel: (514) 272-4566

AUSTRALIA

PREMDWEEP RAJNEESH MEDITATION CENTER
64 Fullarton Rd., Norwood, S.A. 5067 Tel: 08-423388

SATPRAKASH RAJNEESH MEDITATION CENTER
108 Oxford Street, Darlinghurst 2010, N.S.W.
Tel: (02) 336570

SAHAJAM RAJNEESH SANNYAS ASHRAM
6 Collie Street, Fremantle 6160, W.A.
Tel: (09) 336-2422

SVARUP RAJNEESH MEDITATION CENTER
169 Elgin St., Carlton 3053, Victoria Tel: 347-6274

AUSTRIA

PRADEEP RAJNEESH MEDITATION CENTER
Siebenbrunnenfeldgasse 4, 1050 Vienna Tel: 542-860

BELGIUM

VADAN RAJNEESH MEDITATION CENTER
Platte-Lo-Straat 65, 3200 Leuven (Kessel-Lo)
Tel: 016/25-1487

BRAZIL

PRASTHAN RAJNEESH MEDITATION CENTER
R. Paulos Matos 121, Rio de Janeiro, R.J. 20251
Tel: 222-9476

PURNAM RAJNEESH MEDITATION CENTER
Caixa Postal 1946, Porto Alegre, RS 90000

CHILE

SAGARO RAJNEESH MEDITATION CENTER
Golfo de Darien 10217, Las Condas, Santiago
Tel: 472476

DENMARK

ANAND NIKETAN RAJNEESH MEDITATION CENTER
Strøget, Frederiksberggade 15, 1459 Copenhagen K
Tel: (01) 139940

EAST AFRICA

ANAND NEED RAJNEESH MEDITATION CENTER
Kitisuru Estate, P.O. Box 72424, Nairobi, Kenya
Tel: 582600

FRANCE

PRADIP RAJNEESH MEDITATION CENTER
23 Rue Cecile, Maisons Alfoet, 94700 Paris
Tel: 3531190

GREAT BRITAIN

KALPTARU RAJNEESH MEDITATION CENTER
28 Oak Village, London NW5 4QN Tel: (01) 267-8304

MEDINA RAJNEESH NEO-SANNYAS COMMUNE
Herringswell, Bury St. Edmunds, Suffolk 1P28 6SW
Tel: (0638) 750234

HOLLAND

DE STAD RAJNEESH NEO-SANNYAS COMMUNE
Kamperweg 80-86 8191 KC Heerde Tel: 05207-1261

GRADA RAJNEESH NEO-SANNYAS COMMUNE
Prins Hendrikstraat 64, 1931 BK Egmond aan Zee
Tel: 02206-4114

INDIA

RAJNEESHDHAM NEO-SANNYAS COMMUNE
17 Koregaon Park, Poona 411 001, MS Tel: 28127

RAJ YOGA RAJNEESH MEDITATION CENTER
C5/44 Safdarjang Development Area, New Delhi 100 016
Tel: 654533

ITALY

MIASTO RAJNEESH NEO-SANNYAS COMMUNE
Podere S. Giorgio, Cotorniano, 53010 Frosini (Siena)
Tel: 0577-960124

VIVEK RAJNEESH MEDITATION CENTER
Via San Marco 40/4, 20121 Milan Tel: 659-5632

JAPAN

SHANTIYUGA RAJNEESH MEDITATION CENTER
Sky Mansion 2F, 1-34-1 Ookayama, Meguro-ku, Tokyo
152
Tel: (03) 724-9631

UTSAVA RAJNEESH MEDITATION CENTER
2-9-8 Hattori-Motomachi, Toyonaki-shi, Osaka 561
Tel: 06-863-4246

NEW ZEALAND

SHANTI NIKETAN RAJNEESH MEDITATION CENTER
115 Symonds Street, Auckland Tel: 770-326

PUERTO RICO

BHAGWATAM RAJNEESH MEDITATION CENTER
Calle Sebastian 208 (Altos), Viejo San Juan, PR 00905
Tel: 725-0593

SPAIN

SARVOGEET RAJNEESH MEDITATION CENTER
C. Titania 55, Madrid, 33 Tel: 200-0313

SWEDEN

DEEVA RAJNEESH MEDITATION CENTER
Surbrunnsgatan 60, 11327 Stockholm Tel: (08) 327788

SWITZERLAND

GYANDIP RAJNEESH MEDITATION CENTER
Baumackerstr. 42, 8050 Zurich Tel: (01) 312 1600

WEST GERMANY

ANAND SAGAR RAJNEESH MEDITATION CENTER
Lutticherstr. 33/35, 5000 Cologne 1 Tel: 0221-517199

BAILE RAJNEESH NEO-SANNYAS COMMUNE
Karolinenstr. 7-9, 2000 Hamburg 6 Tel: (040) 432140

RAJNEESHSTADT NEO-SANNYAS COMMUNE
Schloss Wolfsbrunnen, 3446 Meinhard-Schwebda
Tel: (05651) 70044

SATDHARMA RAJNEESH MEDITATION CENTER
Klenzestr. 41, 8000 Munich 5 Tel: (089) 269-077

DÖRFCHEN RAJNEESH NEO-SANNYAS COMMUNE
Urbanstr. 64, 1000 Berlin 61 Tel: (030) 691-7917

the Orange Book

These are methods to play with, to help you to celebrate the exploration into yourselves. Unique in their originality and utter simplicity, these meditations reflect Bhagwan's understanding and insight into man's essential nature, and provide the world with a synthesis between the Eastern meditative approach and Western psychological techniques. Dance, shake, gaze in a mirror, beat a pillow, hum, sing, anything that will take you beyond the mind. . .

ISBN 0-88050-697-0   Paperback $3.95

The Meditation Techniques of:

Bhagwan Shree Rajneesh